Saints and Rascals

By
Geraldine DiNardo

TABLE OF CONTENTS

Geri DiNardo's book of portraits of guests at the Mustard Seed Catholic Worker, Worcester, is a treasure. It is a truly authentic biography of a diverse community, including men and women who offer their services every day. I am in awe of Geri's ability to convey the blessings – the generosity and achievement – that the Mustard Seed represents, as a gift to all of us, over four decades.

Michael True
Professor Emeritus of English
Assumption College

Michael True is a long time fellow traveler of the Catholic Worker movement. He spent over thirty years teaching English at Assumption College. He is the author of 10 books including *Homemade Social Justice, People Power: Fifty Peacemakers & Their Communities and An Energy Field More Powerful than War*. He is a co-founder of the New England Catholic Peace Fellowship and The Center for Nonviolent Solutions.

Catholic Worker community life is filled with stories, usually featuring encounters among a rich diversity of people. Geri DiNardo introduces us to a few memorable characters who dropped into the Worcester Catholic Worker over four decades. Her stories of "saints and rascals", like her lifetime of generous service, are sacraments of love, pointing to and making present the love that is God's Holy Spirit.

David J. O'Brien,
Professor Emeritus of History and Loyola Professor of Roman Catholic Studies at the College of the Holy Cross

David O'Brien is an eminent American Catholic historian and the author of many books including *The Renewal of American Catholicism, Public Catholicism and Isaac Hecker*. David is a co-founder of the New England Catholic Peace Fellowship and the Center for Religion, Culture and Ethics at the College of the Holy Cross

4

Dedication

Rita Corbin and Michael Boover

This little work is dedicated to Rita Corbin, Catholic Worker artist and generally marvelous woman, now deceased. It was Rita who first encouraged me to write on the lives of these wonderful people. Also, I wish to dedicate this work to Michael Boover, who, though younger than I, has been my Catholic Worker mentor for more than 40 years. Finally, I remember all who have touched or somehow been touched by the Mustard Seed itself. Bless us all.

Geri DiNardo

The Mustard Seed Catholic Worker
House of Hospitality
c.1974, drawing by Dan Osterman

PREFACE

The Mustard Seed, a storefront and later a Catholic Worker House of Hospitality, has experienced a number of people who took the helm starting with Frank and Shawn and ending, thus far, with Donna who has served the poor for over these past thirty years. This little work represents merely a slice of time in the life of the Mustard Seed and primarily, but not solely, it represents those who were a part of the Seed in the first ten years. Michael and I are fond of saying that "the first ten years were hard". And, they were hard. But also there were good times thanks to many good people who kept us seeking and growing. It is my wish to have represented here these good times and these good people as they were and for some few, as they still are.

The kingdom of God is like a mustard seed... the smallest of all the seeds but becomes the biggest so that the birds of the air shelter in its branches.

FOREWORD

Geraldine DiNardo and I have shared a pilgrim path for over four decades now and we are still "on pilgrimage" as Dorothy Day oft described her experience of Catholic Worker life. Geri and I were involved at the fledgling

"Mustard Seed" storefront begun in 1972 as a "community living room" at 195 Pleasant Street in inner city Worcester, Massachusetts. We were signatories in 1974 on the deed of the first "Mustard Seed House of Hospitality" at 93 Piedmont Street. We opened a free kitchen that fed many daily, distributed food and clothing donations and provided a roof over the head for those in need of shelter. The house was also a place to pray and clarify thought in the Worker tradition. Geri and I purchased a second "community" house at 9 Merrick Street" when our community's membership was bursting at the seams. That house, now happily named "Saint Vincent de Paul House," today serves as a quiet home for low-income Latino families thanks to "Matthew 25," a Jesuit-inspired effort to rehabilitate houses for long-term occupancy. Geri still lives on Merrick Street- she for many years now at # 29, another house of hospitality settled by our friend, Richard "Koz" Kozlowski, once the farmer and all-around workman at the "House of Ammon" Catholic Worker Farm in the North County village of Hubbardston. My wife Diane and I currently live on a small yet "countryish" urban farm here on the inside edge of the city, an albeit modest but hopeful expression of the CW's "Green Revolution." We are all still committed to having some part in the Catholic Worker vision- to cult (the life of the spirit); to culture (the life of the mind) and to cultivation (manual labor and the doing of the works of mercy). Our lives remain forever joined because of our shared hopes and experiences in the movement over these many decades. By the grace of God and the generosity of many people we continue to pray and work together. We are indeed a very blessed people!

Geri and I, along with other dear Catholic Worker kin, took to heart the radical message of the Gospel. Adhering to cherished Catholic Worker values, we strove, even if imperfectly, to do what followers of Jesus ideally should. We endured trials galore and suffered failures too; yet we also enjoyed rare, grace-filled and happy times that were profoundly consoling. As Geri and I age, she in her early seventies and me in my mid-sixties as of this writing, we find ourselves looking back over our proverbial shoulders. Our reminiscing has led us to recall frightening episodes we'd prefer not to revisit. Yet there is healing found in remembering painful parts of our history as there is in recalling the brightest episodes that were so clearly life-giving and renewing in those early years. This book appropriately looks at the sad as well as the glad.

Life is a grand mystery and for us as Christians there is legitimate difficulty in assessing it all. My sense is the Paschal Mystery is central to any deep reviewing of these memories. A special thread that runs throughout- shadow and light alternatingly shaping our life together in the Mystical Body of Christ. There is much to learn from our past. There were matters to celebrate and reasons for repentance; moral messes and redemptive surprises and there are lessons still to be learned. Improvement perennially beckons for more room! There is a bright future we pray.

In these profiles of rascals and saints alike, we can profit from taking good measure of how we can be combinations of both- yet still all called (as best we can in the light of grace bestowed) to live lives inspired by and maybe even comparable to God's officially holy ones, the saints!

Geri has herein crafted lovely portraits of some of the memorable people we came to share our lives and fortunes with, she providing a window through which to view and review that "something special" about our own "Beloved Community's" travails and glories! The reader is in for a treat for Geri writes straight from the heart as to better let the reader in on her holy secrets. Here are "characters with character" who moved us and whose stories deserve her most tender telling. Geri's writing shines a light on the radical faith and generosity at the social heart of the Catholic Worker movement but also tells us much about her personal faith and kindness. Geri loved and still loves the people she wrote and writes about. These are truly love stories! Geri has written a veritable history of the early days of our Catholic Worker experiment. Deeply personal and insightful, Geri captures something of each individual's struggles and gifts that- added up- made for our graced gathering and indeed still make for our rare combination of love-hungry souls who are yet still sating the pangs of physical hunger and lifting the burden of loneliness at our common table. Together we each made a contribution to the unique communal expression that was and is and hopefully will be the Mustard Seed.

The special graces brought to Geraldine and I and our Catholic Worker companions through our beloved guests and each other at the house of hospitality constitute a mystical history of the house, a most blessed history if we are to take seriously Peter Maurin's and Dorothy Day's sense of things. As such, prose does some justice but limited justice. So Geri adds a fitting poetic summation at the end of each profile as to more fully lift up a particular person in the eye of her mind and especially her heart. We are further enriched by her appreciations thereby for in her sight of the poor or gifted other, she also sees and celebrates the *Christus* who so identifies with and loves them.

Enjoy these portraits and poetic commentaries for they speak of our experiment's part in the Mystical Body of Christ in our own time and place and of the Ultimate Mystery we were privileged to have some share in through the days and nights spent in that old house. Bless you Geri for writing of that Grand Mystery and bless you dear readers as you celebrate with us a heritage and a promise-struggles and joys aplenty- in these memories that in the sharing still urge us forward to that blessed "vision that still has its time."

Michael Boover
Annunciation House of Worcester

ACKNOWLEDGEMENTS

It is with particular gratitude that I render my thanks to my editors Margaret Farren, David Webster, Michael Boover, Tim Morse, and David O'Brien; to my readers: Diane Boover, Stephanie Moran, Terry Brady, Jane Fraier, Annette Rafferty, Mike True and my sister, Joan Cumming.

I wish to give thanks to my typing assistant and editor, Carlene Carpenter, without whom this work would not have been completed.

Finally, thanks to all the many others who have in any way contributed to this work.

A BRIEF HISTORY

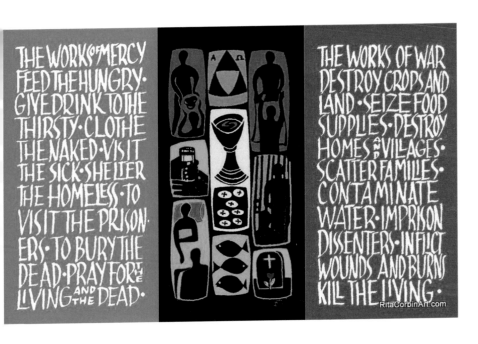

The works of mercy rather than the works of war - -
a drawing by Rita Corbin

THE CATHOLIC WORKER IN

WORCESTER AND ITS ENVIRONS

Some of the information following was gleaned from papers written by Michael Harank[1], at the time a student at Holy Cross College, and Michael Boover.[2]

---

[1] "A History of the First Catholic Worker Community in Worcester, MA 1938-1940"
[2] The Catholic Worker in Worcester" The Catholic Radical June/July 2001 Edition

The Mustard Seed did not emerge from a vacuum. No, there was a history. The Catholic Worker had its beginnings on May 1, 1933, founded by Peter Maurin and Dorothy Day in New York City. Much has been said about its aims and purposes. I sometimes think I have a more simplistic mind. For me, the Catholic Worker is about doing the works of mercy at a personal sacrifice: doing the works of mercy rather than the works of war.

In April of 1938, a small group of Catholic Workers from the Boston area came to speak in Worcester. This prompted a group of people to announce that the first CW meeting in Worcester would be held on the feast of the Ascension. The first CW in Worcester had begun. The group decided to rent the top two floors of a 2 ½ story wood frame house at 25 Austin Street from a Mr. Washburn who constructed artificial limbs in his shop on the first floor. Soon, there was soup (boiled fish heads and potato soup). Ultimately one hundred to two hundred were fed daily. The house was named Matt Talbot House, after an Irishman who sought sobriety amidst great difficulty, winning the battle through the grace of God.

Soon, a farm was bought in Upton, a small town close enough to Worcester. In June, Dorothy came with the $50 down-payment and the farm was born – in Peter Maurin's words, "the agronomic university". Men came from the city to the farm to help with the work and to seek respite from city life. St. Benedict's farm, as it came to be called, still lives. Carl Paulson, an early Catholic Worker, conscientious objector and stained glass window maker, lives through his son and grandson who still practice Carl's type of artistry there. The Matt Talbot House experiment lasted for two very moving years, ultimately closing primarily due to marriages within the community. It was a great run. These were the beginnings of the Catholic Worker in Worcester.

About 33 years after the inception of Matt Talbot was born the House of Ammon in Hubbardston, a small rural area about 20 miles from the city of Worcester, founded by three rather unlikely candidates: Fr. Bernie, sometimes referred to as the Catholic Worker priest, Koz, Bernie's disciple, and Jeannette, middle-aged at the time, the parish sacristan. The three, all holy people, made it a policy to treat all who came to the door as Christ, refusing no one. For this, they paid dearly. Not all who came shared the same love and respect for one another. For example, there was the winter day that some guests found themselves rather chilly. Jeannette and others were away. These few guests chopped Jeannette's bed and burned it in the stove for heat. Then there were the strawberries. Jeannette's hand grown, picked and preserved strawberries were stolen and sold for a few pennies at the town center. These things can wear one down. It has been said that the strawberries were the last straw for Jeannette. But there were many great graces at the House of Ammon. We from the Mustard Seed (more about this later) attended beautiful weekly Mass and inspiring homilies preached by Fr. Bernie. Mass was followed by communal dinner. The House of Ammon endured for seven years in both joy and sorrow. Then, fire…the burning of the house, the loss of a life. This was the story of one Catholic Worker house, the House of Ammon named for the famed Catholic Worker, Ammon Hennacy, and some who tried mightily to do God's will.

About the same time as the House of Ammon, there came forth two young Holy Cross students. Frank Kartheiser and Shawn Donovan, who were taken with the anti-war movement. They wanted to answer the works of war with the works of mercy. To this end they opened the Mustard Seed Catholic Worker storefront (c. 1971). This was the second of the Catholic Worker organisms to grace the City of Worcester. The Mustard Seed storefront was really a community living room, with chairs, card tables, cards and good company – a success by all accounts. The storefront lasted sometime over a year with camaraderie during the week, and a trek to the Hubbardston farm for Mass and communal dining on Sundays.

Oh, the storefront had its idiosyncrasies: liquor hidden in the back of the toilet to stay cold; homemade soup brought in and left on the radiator to stay hot. Then came the fire. It was just a small fire in the trash bin but large enough to cause the landlord to order the Mustard Seed closed and out of the building. The end of one era, the beginning of another as Michael, Frank and I began meeting with one or two others to talk about opening a Catholic Worker House of Hospitality, a continuation, so to speak, of the Mustard Seed storefront.

****

But before forging on further in the life of the Mustard Seed, I wish to introduce the third of the Catholic Worker houses in the city of Worcester. In 1986 the St. Francis and Therese House of Hospitality was opened, spear-headed by Claire and Scott. In 1987 a fire caused a move to 52 Mason Street. They are a courageous couple having raised four children, housing and feeding a modest number of guests, leading many demonstrations and publishing a beautiful paper, "The Catholic Radical". Scott and Claire have traveled the world in the name of justice and peace. They have done much, much more and they continue to do so. We love and admire them.

****

Returning to the Mustard Seed saga:

We met, and we met, and we met. We thought we had found a house on Hudson Street -- to no avail. By now I had resigned myself that a Catholic Worker house was not to be. After three months, finally, a call. There was a house at 93 Piedmont Street, looking promising. A friend, Dan, was asked to check the house. It was solid. Then, the purchase. Some little girls sold Mustard Seed keychains to raise money for the down payment. Michael agreed to sign for ownership. I, taking his lead as I often did, agreed to sign also. Anne, the owner, chose not to go through a bank. Just a modest monthly payment over 15 years. These conditions were suitable for us. And so, we took over ownership of the Mustard Seed House of Hospitality at 93 Piedmont Street.

The Mustard Seed House of Hospitality officially opened on March 25, 1974. Mass was said by friends: three priests: Fr. Bernie Gilgun, Fr. Frank Scollen (later to become Monsignor) and Fr. John Burke. There were many guests who came: soon some stayed to eat and some merely stayed. Generally speaking, the food was hearty, although I do remember one meal of lettuce soup – scarcity of food.

Fridays were tough. I do have a recollection of our friend Debbie B. who volunteered to cook on Fridays. Today I marvel at how she could make a dinner – "something out nothing" each week, and I am ashamed at how we quickly scurried away when Debbie came to take over. There were difficulties, but there were joys also – such as the weekend retreat at which our beloved prayer plant came into full bloom. I did have feelings of being married to all in the community and the need to get along with all. It was difficult. There was the day Michael played the St. Francis in the buff, on the third floor porch in the rain. The Mustard Seed was a far cry from the papier-mâché flowers and lovely table cloths that I had envisioned.

In 1984 the Mustard Seed was destroyed by fire. Only old Joe was hurt. Thankfully, he lived to tell the tale. The Mustard Seed was rebuilt as a soup kitchen through the generosity of the people of Worcester County and beyond. It continues through the generosity of hundreds, if not thousands, of volunteer cooks, servers, donors and others, and has served hundreds, and I dare say thousands, of guests. Peace and joy to all who passed this path. Following are short stories of some of these brave souls and others, not so brave.

THE GUESTS

Charlie Schlitz

Charlie Schlitz
c. 1978 – a drawing by Dan Osterman
Charlie Schlitz little black man
who does what he wants to
but only when he can.

I do not recall how Charlie first landed at the Mustard Seed. I have been told that he arrived with a key. "This is the key to my room upstairs." "But Charlie, we have no locks in this house". "No, this is the key to my room". With this, Charlie was ushered in as a guest of the Mustard Seed. He was to live there with us for the rest of his life.

The little ditty above about the little black man, was posted at the head of his bed and there it remained. Charlie became among the most helpful of the Mustard Seed guests and a true member of the family.

And he was strong, very small but very strong. There was no better help than a physically strong person at the Mustard Seed, with all the comings and goings of the food and the farming work at St. Joseph's Abbey. I was told that he could tend a row of vegetables faster than any of the crew.

His spirituality was noteworthy – he prayed aloud primarily when under the influence of liquor. But still there was a mysticism that it is not to be denied. He spoke in tongues as far as we could determine, and we all appreciated his holiness whether or not tainted by the drink.

He frequently referred to himself as "The Great Father", and we, too, thought of him in this light. He was the Mustard Seed dishwasher among his many talents - a great dishwasher - he was a good worker in any capacity.

But the day did come when we had to implore Charlie to please use *hot* water when washing the dishes.

And Charlie was the fire marshal. It was he who walked the floors at night, checking for unextinguished cigarettes and other potential fire hazards. It was Charlie who was my right hand man when other community members were away on pilgrimages or other missions.

Yes, he was a gem! A shining star among the stars.

Charlie eventually became ill and even this had its comical aspect. On one occasion, I went with him to the emergency room at City Hospital. As is customary, the nurse greeted us at the station. I was just about to utter his name, "Charlie Schlitz", to the nurse and he said, "James Salters". I was astonished. "Charlie, what's this?", I asked. "James Salters", he repeated. Seems that Charlie had been a striker for the Schlitz bottling company and had acquired the moniker "Charlie Schlitz", and so James Salters became known by all as Charlie Schlitz. Known by all by this name, except it appears in formal settings – like hospitals. There, he was James Salters. Yes, we learn something new every day.

Charlie was eventually diagnosed with stomach cancer. And, yes, there was even at least one comical event around this – not to be forgotten by me, anyway, after all these years. Michael, Francis D. and I were visiting with Charlie in his hospital room. At one point, Charlie let out a wail (in pain, I suppose). Francis D. raised his voice: "Charlie", he scolded, "be quiet." Was it the naiveté, the innocence of the poor? Was it callousness? Francis gave Charlie what was to be his last scolding.

And later, he died.

Probably the most memorable moments around Charlie Schlitz came after he died. I was living in a room about ½ mile from the Mustard Seed, and word of Charlie's death came to me. Charlie liked to dress fancy, so for his burial we had cleaned his suit.

Margie and Ray appeared at my room and the three of us put his outfit together as he would have wanted it: cleaned suit, polished shoes, necktie, etc. – complete outfit.

I was moved by these small acts of kindness for a beloved who had passed. This was for me a new twist on the work of mercy, "to bury the dead."

Charlie's funeral was a great event for the "little black man who does what he wants to" – filled with monks and priests, his birth daughter and his friends.

CHARLIE

Oh, the little black man

Strong.

Vigilant.

Holy.

You kept me safe

When I was unable

To care for myself.

Thank you.

You spoke of God

When I doubted.

Thank you.

You came back

When sent away.

Thank you.

EARL THE PEARL

Earl, by the window   7/28/78   Mike Boover

Earl by his favorite window
1978 linoleum block print by Michael Boover

I remember how Earl C. came to live at the Mustard Seed. He had been homeless in downtown Worcester and met a young evangelical friend of Michael. Danny suggested to Earl to come to 93 Piedmont Street and there he might find a home with us. Earl came and there he did find a home.

Earl was somewhat unusual with his long hair and white beard, looking a lot like Tolstoy. While he was up and about, he loved to sit by the window in the Mustard Seed kitchen.

"Earl the Pearl" we called him jokingly. But soon this nickname turned very serious, when to me, he became the Pearl of Great Price.

There were days, many days, when the work became frustrating, very frustrating. At these times, I would turn, walk upstairs and find Earl in his room. I said nothing of my state of mind. However, almost mysteriously in a very short time, Earl would begin to regale me with stories of his adventures in homelessness.

He often slept in downtown doorways at night. Occasionally he got lucky to find a door to a building open and perhaps would sleep in the bathtub of the shared bathroom.

There were stories of riding the rails as a younger man, too. But as he grew and somehow settled in Worcester, he learned a certain art of doing something to get himself jailed so as to be out of the cold in winter. While living on the streets food often came by way of a Table Talk pie truck left open for delivery.

Yes, Earl would launch into these and other stories of life on the streets and I, listening, would slowly begin to feel again that the Mustard Seed life was still worth living. We were glad to have him in the family.

A friend of his helped him to get an assistance check and so he became a bit wealthier than the other housemates. Charlie, who lived in the adjoining room from Earl, became his friend and his "runner". Yes, there were plenty of fried chicken boxes in Earl's room and, truth be told, plenty of liquor bottles, too. Charlie became ill and passed into eternity in June, 1980.

Earl grew weaker and refused the hospital. Two months after the death of his beloved friend, Earl, too, entered the heavenly gates.

But this is not the end of the story of Charlie and Earl. I had the privilege of making arrangements at the funeral home for Earl's burial. Dear Henry, the most generous funeral director, was very happy to hear that Earl's "estate" included some funds to help pay for his burial. Plans were made. There would be a funeral plot for Earl somewhere in Notre Dame Cemetery.

Well, long-story-short, on the day of his burial, we were led to the plot. Hard to believe, unknown and unplanned, Earl's casket lay in death exactly next to Charlie, his friend in life. Yes, it lay in death, directly next to Charlie's burial plot – unplanned and unexplained. There are no coincidences with God.

An addendum to Earl's story:

There is a part of Earl's life at the Mustard Seed which cannot be left untold:

Mike, Richard, and Joanne had left on pilgrimage to Europe. I happened to be at the hospital with a guest of the house. Meanwhile, back at the house, a man was nearly killed, coming remarkably close to being shot in the head by a very tough belligerent guest.

Very soon after, I called upon a small group of people. I refer to them as the elders – the Demers, the Goulets, Fr. Frank Scollen, Fr. Cy Le Beau – for advice and affirmation. I felt it too dangerous for the guests to continue to be housed at the Mustard Seed. And so, with the approval of the elders, I closed the house until the other community members might return. It fell upon me to tell all in the house that they had to leave, at least temporarily.

Now, here's where Earl comes in. After being told the news, he was seen by me walking down the stairs with a heavy, black coat over his arm. Mind you, this was August.

"Where will you go, Earl?" I asked. "Oh, back to the weeds, Geri." Now, it wasn't so much what Earl said that caught my attention. It was the way he said it with no anger, no malice, no disdain - no hint of, "how could you do this to me again?" Just acceptance, beautiful acceptance. I thought quickly about what was happening. And quickly, I made my decision. I wouldn't, shouldn't, do it. And my mind was made up. "Earl, I'm asking you not to go. You can stay on with us as a family."

And so he did stay on as a dear member of the family and so he died with us and was miraculously buried as described above with his brother Charlie next to him.

This is the story of how Earl became a permanent member of the Mustard Seed family.

EARL

Pearl of great price

The cold

The homeless

You bore such dignity, found a home with us

It was you who brought us there

Home to ourselves

A more lasting peace

Amid the chaos

You, always, the old man

With the jewels.

"DEEP SIX"

I have no recollection of how John first arrived at the Mustard Seed. It seems he was always there. He was most likely, if not most definitely, an alcoholic. So, he probably came to us looking for a home. And so he found – not forever, but for a long, long while, a home – and, to my knowledge, he was sober all the while.

John was not like either Charlie or Earl, in that he did not serve a particular function in the community, such as making food runs to the sisters in Wrentham like Charlie, nor regaling us with uplifting stories like Earl. No, John was more the ombudsmen, the jack-of-all (Mustard Seed) trades. He spent much time on the first floor, so often was the first to greet the guests.

The young people were not among his favorites. Thus, he was fond of saying of them and other unwanteds, "just give 'em the deep six." And John did have somewhat of a temper, not an overt temper mind you, but a sort of covert temper, looking something like this: arms out to side about eight inches away from the body, face red, very red. When one noted this stance, it was best to leave John to himself for a time, lest one be in danger of being given the famous "deep six".

Perhaps I am a bit mistaken in saying that John had no official capacity in the community. Yes, he was ombudsmen, but he was also the Mustard Seed ambassador to the neighborhood. First, there was Aggie, widow and our cherished neighbor. It was John who mowed her lawn, trimmed the hedges, helped her in numerous ways and especially walked Jake, her over-sized dog. Being aware of the temptation of money, Aggie rewarded John with coffee or muffins and warm friendship.

But John was ambassador to the neighborhood for there was lawn mowing, hedge clipping and snow shoveling all around, and the neighborhood looked so good for John's careful attention.

He was by no means warm and fuzzy, but he was a good and loyal man and the Mustard Seed was all the better for having known him. It is unclear to me exactly when he left the Mustard Seed, perhaps after the fire.

Word came to us that he was living with or near his sister, several towns away from Worcester. We never saw him again.

We loved him.

JOHN

Rough and gruff you were.

For those who don't conform

Just "give them the deep six."

Out of many, it was you

Who were so helpful to others.

Complete strangers,

Doubtful you knew their names.

As for Big Jake,

It was you with your kindness,

It was you who allowed

An elderly widow

To keep her beloved dog.

We cannot think of the Mustard Seed,

Without thinking of you.

Thank you from all the neighborhood.

You came a stranger.

You left a brother.

MAMA BEA

Mama Bea, formally known as Beatrice G, was nothing, if not gracious always, and she was nothing, if not hospitable, always. She presided over the third floor kitchen.

Mama Bea arrived at the Mustard Seed with her rather large but friendly dog, Pupsin, in tow, looking for all the world like a larger-than-life Mary Poppins. Only this image of her and a few vague recollections remain.

She was most kind and good and hospitable, especially to priests, and of the priests, she was most kind and good and hospitable to Fr. Bernie – "…a cup of tea Father….something to eat, Father." A kind of "mi casa, su casa" hospitality.

I have pored over this next issue long and hard. How to pose it delicately? Why not delete it completely? Well, the truth is, it was such an integral part of her story. The truth is….the truth is….Mama Bea came with lice, plenty of lice. I was aware of this situation and so made an appointment that she might see a professional at Family Health. I should have seen, but did not foresee, the difficulties that such a visit might provoke.

And so, we walked to Family Health. I was not wanting the critters to take up residence in my car. Mama Bea and I made the trek to the clinic. We were invited into the reception office. The questions began. Mama Bea momentarily lowered her head over the desk. The lice cascade onto the desk. It seemed that chaos ensued. I do not remember the rest of that visit; I know only that I got a call the next day from Family Health clinic…"please, would I take care of the problem before bringing Beatrice back again."

Needless to say, lice took control of the Mustard Seed and there was plenty of Kwell all around. Thus the bugs were dispatched. The sequel to this particular story is that Mama Bea, who it seems was water phobic, was aided in a tub bath by two angels, Sara and Aline.

Mama Bea continued as her most hospitable self and Mustard Seed life went on as usual with her as reigning queen of the third floor kitchen. Mama Bea eventually became sick. She was taken to City Hospital. We did not see her alive again. I do not have a clear recollection of this, but I believe there was a "No Visitors" order on her at the hospital.

We somehow heard word of her death. Funeral at 7:00a.m. We were thankful to do this last of the works of mercy for her – to bury the dead. We fondly remember her.

Mama Bea

There you were
Mama Bea,
A Mary Poppins.
A cup of tea
You proffered
To all
Who came.
The works of mercy
A reality
In you,
For us to see.

Mrs. Christ

Mrs. Fish and Joe Goulet

FISH KENNEDY FISH

Undoubtedly, the most colorful of all the colorful Mustard Seed characters is Mrs. Elizabeth Fish Kennedy Fish. I first met Mrs. Fish at the Mustard Seed storefront on Pleasant Street. I will say only that our first visit was intimidating.

Marilyn D., her married name, was strikingly beautiful in her younger days and remained so throughout life. She rejected her name, Marilyn, and woe be to the person who dared to call her thus. How deeply was Mrs. Fish's rejection of her former identity can be seen in the following story:

Elizabeth (Fish) had a birth son, Billy D. Billy, a good and kind young man, visited his mother at the Mustard Seed often. Despite her vagaries into the sometimes unintelligible banter of schizophrenia, the two developed what appeared to be a solid mother/son relationship.

I do not know if Mrs. Fish rationally discerned the discrepancy in Billy bearing the D. name, so rejected by her in the past. What to do? What to do was to change Billy's last name, make it more congruent. Mrs. Fish began to call Billy D. by her chosen, by his "correct" or "corrected" name.

Ever after until his untimely death, Billy D. was called by his dear mother, re-named so to speak the young

Billy Fish – and so he accepted his new name as clearly and dearly as to be his own given name.

The story of Mrs. Fish can be viewed as the story of a neighborhood, the Piedmont Street/Merrick Street neighborhood. She was safe there, and to my knowledge she was never hurt, abused, or harassed by anyone in the neighborhood.

She made friends also with Gert K. Gert had lost three of her six children to death in separate incidents. Mrs. Fish lost Billy and at least one daughter.

The following stories tell how she was accepted as an integral part of the comings and goings of all that happened here. Here she belonged. Here she was safe and there were those of us who hoped that she would stay within the confines of the Piedmont Street neighborhood.

Gert was a clerk at the West Side Pharmacy (about three blocks from the Seed). She was good and kind to all despite the heartbreaking and tragic loss of her three children.

Mrs. Fish, too, had suffered loss of her children. Her dear Billy (Fish) somehow fell from a porch to his death in his early 20's and she also had lost a daughter, murdered in Boston.

There was a palpable bond between Gert and Mrs. Fish, unconscious perhaps, but nonetheless a bond. Some would say a mutual compassion, a mutual understanding of a mother's loss, a sympatico of one with the other.

And there were other stories. For instance, there is the one about the rescue by the Pickle Barrel boys. The

Pickle Barrel, a popular local restaurant, was a second home to Mrs. Fish. She was frequently seen there bussing tables or sweeping floors. Fortunately for her, and all, she somehow managed to get hold of the Pickle Barrel phone number.

Lucky for her, because one fine day found her lost and several towns away. (How she happened to land there was never revealed). Aha! – the phone number. Yes, she managed to find a phone and call the Pickle Barrel. And yes, the Pickle Barrel workers left their work, got in their car, and drove the several towns away, somehow finding Mrs. Fish, rescuing her, really, and returned her safely to the familiar neighborhood. The words of the song, "We are Family" comes to mind.

There were many other aspects of Mrs. Fish, yet to be discussed. Perhaps you are wondering how it was that Mrs. Fish came to the Mustard Seed in the first place. In some ways, she was always there. The house belonged to a relative and we were told she visited there when she was young.

She later took up residence in the Mustard Seed house, a little at a time, so to speak. First, she came to the dining room for a time: then, sleeping on the dining room benches – but only for a little while and leaving much before dawn and finally, an all-nighter. After many nights asleep on the hard benches, Mrs. Fish was asked to move in. And so she did and she became a beloved member of the Mustard Seed family.

It must not be misconstrued. She was not always sweet and lovely. Her personality could "turn on a dime" as some would say, and she could become surly and angry. An example: once when something riled her, a chair was hurled at me. It was caught almost in mid-air by dearest Charlie, and life went on as usual.

There was the time when she insulted the visiting Bishop, "You're not the Bishop, I'm the Bishop". There were the times when she was asked to leave the West Side Pharmacy and the Pickle Barrel, each in their turn, for her uttering foul-mouthed schizophrenic banter in front of the customers. Of course she was always welcomed back, for, yes, we were family in this neighborhood.

Mrs. Fish often referred to "her babies", "killing my babies, babies in the walls etc." and woe-be-tide any who did not accept the reality of their existence.

She was multi-talented as well as multi-faceted. She was an artist, really. She gave new meaning to the words: "to read the hand-writing on the wall." Yes, she did much writing on the walls of the Mustard Seed and on her hand-fashioned clothing. Beyond this, though, Mrs. Fish was a great friend of the *Magic Marker* and some of these works of her art still exist today.

Also, she was thought to be a seamstress in her younger years and there is certainly evidence of this in her Mustard Seed years. Mrs. Fish was a fashion plate – a new outfit every day. I suspect that she never wore the same outfit twice – all gorgeous, all hand-sewn and all desperately outlandish with their hand-written messages.

There is a sewing story that must be told: Carol L. lived with Mrs. Fish at the Mustard Seed Merrick Street house and thought perhaps Mrs. Fish needed a new bedspread for her little single bed. Thus, she bought a beautiful new bedspread for Mrs. Fish. Excitedly she gave it, put it on the bed and left the bedroom gleefully for having done a good deed. Two hours later, Mrs. Fish was seen walking out of the house wearing the hand-made bedspread coat. She had hand-sewn it and I suppose was quite proud of herself.

Many of us were beneficiaries of Mrs. Fish's unique creations. I, myself, was given several: blouses/shirts, Christmas outfits, etc. – all hand inscribed with messages only she fully understood.

Another thought about life before Mrs. Fish arrived at the Mustard Seed: it was thought that she lived in abandoned buildings in the area, likely sleeping there during the day. Nightly, she took the long trek to Webster Square Big Boy's (a local all-night restaurant) for coffee and….. It is unclear how Mrs. Fish did afford evening coffee – likely from the kindness of strangers.

Another note on the Mustard Seed life of Mrs. Fish is very significant and personal to me. There was a time in my own later years at the Mustard Seed that I suffered from a mental illness. I took to the bed for an entire month and it was Mrs. Fish, among others of the poor, who ministered to and monitored me that I might not wander.

Yes, over my years, it was the poor who have given me far more than have I given to the poor. We are all wounded healers, I suppose. Some of us are aware of it.

This may be the time to insert the chapter on the Mustard Seed written by Harry Murray in the book, <u>Do Not Neglect</u> Hospitality. We were all given pseudonyms for purpose of anonymity – the pseudonym for Elizabeth Fish Kennedy Fish, the most colorful of all the colorful Mustard Seed characters, she was called.....Mrs. Christ.

Time passed. Her natural family contacted her more often. Mrs. Fish became ill. She took up residence in a local nursing home. I no longer lived at the Mustard Seed, but saw her occasionally. It was Donna, however, who saved the day for Mrs. Fish. It appears that Mrs. Fish had contracted diabetes. The doctor thought it best to amputate a foot. Donna thoroughly disagreed, and made it known that this was not to happen and it did not.

Fish (as she was sometimes called) did grow weaker – not because of the foot, I'm sure – and she passed with both feet intact and connected to her body.

Peace, dear lady. You brightened our life.

Mrs. Fish

Woman of
Many names
Elizabeth, Cleopatra
Mrs. Fish
The name most true
Hidden under layers
Of fashion
Sewn by you
The name most true
Bestowed by a stranger
The name most true.
You, you were Mrs. Christ
For those who have eyes,
Let them see
Who you are:
Mrs. Fish, the Christ

Tommy N.

TOMMY N.

My first recollection of Tommy N. was that of him scooting determinedly on his backside up the three flights of stairs to the third floor living quarters. Tom was a hemophiliac and also suffered from a condition of what appeared to be clubbed or severely deformed feet. At any rate, he was unable to walk and usually used a wheelchair unless it became necessary to move about by other means such as having to travel upwards to the third floor living quarters.

The next situation was to be my first - but not my last - lesson in following or being led to the exhortation of Christ to "go, sell all that you have, and give to the poor..." In my case, "just give what you have to the poor."

When I came to the Mustard Seed, I brought with me my cherished pull-out couch which I had bought with my own money for my little semi-studio apartment after sleeping many months on a mattress over a plywood board and cinder blocks. My couch was offered to Tommy for his sleeping area. Tommy soon had a bout of hemophilia and consequently bled all over my lovely couch. This was the beginning. I cried.

I very much admired Tommy in his perseverance to get where he wanted to go despite his disabilities, both physical and mental. He frequently ran for public office with, it must be said, a rather unorthodox platform. He was well-spoken and also did some political writing. Tom seemed rather proud of his Jewish heritage and I thought, at times, used it against us Christians.

Eventually, he did get to move downstairs to the first floor where he "roomed" with our beloved Dennis. They lived together as brothers and cared for one another.

In time, Tom moved again to our first floor apartment at 9 Merrick Street. Tom was with us there when I suffered the first (and last) of my mental breakdowns at the Mustard Seed. I remember little of this segment of my mental health bout. But, I do remember that Tommy was particularly kind to me. It may be because he himself suffered bi-polar illness, but I prefer to think that it was the genuine warmth of the man that caused him to invite me in, offer me a room and give me kind advice. This I remember fondly of Tommy: that he was kind and good at a time when I craved that kindness and goodness.

But, his life with the Mustard Seed was multi-faceted. When speaking of Tom, there is a story that must be told, though it must be told with great gentleness. It follows.

Tommy was living at 9 Merrick Street and became engaged in a major manic episode. Windows were being systematically broken. Enter Michael, trying to imagine how to stop the destruction. Thinking that if Tommy was out of the wheelchair and on the floor the chaos would stop, Michael attempted to put Tommy to the floor. Alas, a broken ankle! The ankle healed, but rancor ensued. Tommy sued Michael for the injury and thus followed a beautiful story of Christian non-violence and interfaith friendship.

In the spirit of Christian non-violence, Michael attended the court hearings but did not defend himself. Margaret attended the court hearings and did the praying. After a number of court proceedings, Tommy dropped the charges, the friendships resumed, and life at the Mustard Seed continued.

Eventually, Tom returned to live with or near his mother. His condition deteriorated and he died. And this is not quite the end of the story. A grand celebration was held at a local club, in memory of this good and kind and intelligent man who suffered much and gave more.

Tom N.

You were kind
You were good
Irascible in many ways, too.
You were burdened
With many trials.
Pain of mind
And of body.
Some would think you
A grump
With your wry and
Prickly
Sense of humor.
To those who knew you:
Kindness and
Love.

A BROTHER

Of all the fond relationships that were developed at the Mustard Seed, Dennis was my only "little brother." Whether it was his youth, the debilitating effects of the cerebral palsy, or the sweetness of his personality, I always loved him.

I do not recall how he first arrived at the Mustard Seed, but I do recall that Dennis was young, perhaps in his late teens. I'm sure that he had angry moments but I never saw this in him, and to this day, neither have I heard him speak a harsh word of anyone. In short, he was a gem. He was not without faults, but he was a gem.

What I do remember of Dennis is that he lived in a room at the Mustard Seed just off the main dining room with Tommy N. They, too, were brothers.

And Dennis liked to bake bread and did so with great gusto. I can almost see him now in the kitchen and hear him say, "I think I'll bake bread today."

My only other recollections of Dennis at the Mustard Seed did not take place there at all. It was California.

I had "run away" from the Seed to stay for a very long time with some friends in San Jose. Toward the end of my visit, Dennis hitch-hiked his way to California and joined me there. He was a great companion and joined me on my return trip, even doing some of the driving.

Dennis eventually left the Mustard Seed, married (and divorced) and fathered a son whom, it is obvious, he loved beyond measure. During this time Dennis held a job for many years as a taxi cab driver.

We saw very little of him in that time. But eventually, he returned to the neighborhood for dinner, Mass, and prayer services. Some bonds do not break. If Dennis had any fault, perhaps it was his desire to please, to be a friend to all. Certainly not terrible faults.

When Dennis lived, he joined us often. But there were health issues. We tried to live in the day.

Dennis passed from this earth on April 2, 2015. We were grateful for his presence.

Dennis

You are concerned.
"Did you swim this week, Geri?"
"You are too old for your blond hair, Geri".

Does it matter, really?
It matters only
That you care.

It matters only
That things
Make a difference
To you.

It matters only
That you were still here
After
All these years.

You were still my brother.

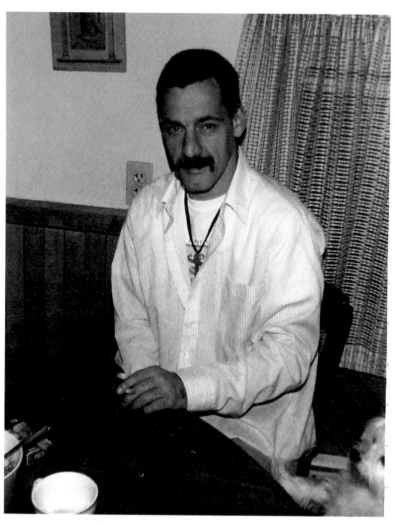

David – my right hand and my left,

my friend and confidant

DAVID

I feel as though I have known David for all of his life. But that is not the whole truth. The truth is that I heard about David when he was a young boy. The truth is there was word that he was the most abused youth ever encountered by the raconteur.

I believe this story because David, himself, often told me of his young life – stories of being beaten with a broomstick, spanked bare-bottomed with a metal spatula, burned with a full pan of boiling water, thrown out of his home and made to walk the 15 (or so) miles back to Worcester, where he was nearly beaten with a hammer and much, much more. David told to me all of these stories and he told them without affect. I loved David. But, I am getting far ahead of myself.

I believe David first appeared on the Mustard Seed scene during Lucky's reign there. I know that he was told to get a "boy's" haircut if he was to stay there, and so he did.

Sometime previous to his arrival at the Mustard Seed, David's girlfriend gave birth to his daughter. He was never again to see this daughter, although there were some phone conversations with her in David's later years. His arrival at the Mustard Seed marked a new chapter in David's life. He became Lucky's right hand, her runner and her enforcer, so-to-speak. It seemed that everyone loved and respected David's quiet strength.

But the abuse of David did not stop in his childhood, nor did it end with his life on the streets, nor by the railroad tracks near which he lived until finally arriving at the Mustard Seed. He was helped to get a monthly government check, but there was a price to be exacted. Most of his check, and sometimes all of it, was to be turned over to his rep payee, leaving him with little or no money remaining for the month.

Also, he broke up many a fight during Lucky's reign at the Mustard Seed, some involving Lucky herself. But David was a friend to all, and is still remembered fondly by the guests. More, later about his capacity as the star dishwasher at the soup kitchen.

By this time, Michael had left the Mustard Seed and I had been gone from there for several years earlier. This period, I believe, was the darkest in the Mustard Seed history. This was the thought of many. Let me say only that times were difficult, though the poor were still fed and cared for. Liquor and drugs abounded.

David was one alcoholic among many and there was much drinking. At this time, Lucky was diagnosed with the dreaded disease of AIDS. It was David who cared for her. Others were afraid. After several months, Lucky signed herself into an AIDS hospice where she lived for another year. David and I visited her on her last day of life on this earth. He was a loyal man.

Lest I forget, it was about this time that David's newest girlfriend, the love of his life, gave birth to his son, Daniel. Though David and Linda never married, she became his dearest one. She happily married someone else, and yet she and David always remained friends, and Daniel remained, until David's death, his shining star.

In the meantime, the Mustard Seed was taken over by a new "director" and David remained as previously alluded, the chief dishwasher. David was often praised as a dishwasher and the groups adored him, for he was courteous and thorough. He loved the job.

But trouble was brewing. According to testimony, told to me by David years after the fact, the following unfortunate circumstance occurred:

He was doing dishes as usual. Someone in the group gave him a compliment. The "director" later reminded him not to take such compliments to heart and "he was nothing to the Mustard Seed." Tempers flared. David let fly a cup of coffee at the "director". Police were called. Eventually David was invited to leave.

To my knowledge, he never returned to the Mustard Seed soup kitchen for the remaining twenty-six plus years of his life.....a great loss to the soup kitchen of a great man and a great dishwasher.

David continued to drink, living at the Mustard Seed-owned #9 Merrick Street. Liquor was flowing freely at the time for David and others.

Finally, Koz appeared, suggesting that David come to Koz's house to "sober up". And so he did. To my knowledge, David never drank again.

David lived the rest of his life at Koz's house. Thus began the last and final chapter of his unusual life.

Sometime after David moved to 29 Merrick Street, I, too, was invited to live there, and elected to live in my lovely little first floor apartment.

David and I became fast friends, and we had also had a financial relationship. I had become his rep payee. I was to verify that his money would be his and his financial needs were met. I fulfilled these duties for nearly 25 years, and to the best of my ability.

And David was a great mimic. How many times one or another of us would ask, "David, do so-and-so." Of course, the most popular of his imitations was Fr. Bernie – right hand on the cheek, left hand holding right elbow, and then, the famous words, "Each and every day is a very hard struggle."

At last, with thanks to Koz for the invitation, David was to find a lasting home, and peace - glorious peace. Here, he found his jobs – housework, floor-washing, cleaning and animal-sitting - jobs which he chose to do. As for me, he became my right-hand and my left, my friend and confidant.

David was mostly, but not completely, non-violent. He feared nothing and no one. There once was a man sitting on the bench in front of a local store and for some reason he began to shout at David. In a flash, the man went from sitting on the bench to having been punched and landing on the ground. Don't mess with David.

Then there was the time at Family Health and Clinic when someone cut into the line for the pharmacy. There was a complaint from the lady standing behind David who immediately picked up the interloper from under the arms, marched with him to the end of the line and unceremoniously dropped him on the floor. Needless to say that from that day on, David's meds were always "ready" for him when he arrived, all the more quickly to be rid of the "troublemaker."

For the next 26 years after leaving the Mustard Seed, David lived at 29 Merrick Street with Koz, Tommy, and later John – a glorious peaceful, and productive life.

I was on the first floor and he was helpful beyond measure with the animals, the trash, the cleaning, making beds and various other helpful missions. David often introduced me in this fashion, "This is Geri. She is like the mother of the house." What I think he really meant, was, "This is Geri. She is like my mother." And I was.

Then came illness. Over the last several years, David grew weaker; difficulties with heart and breathing; unable to do what he was accustomed to do. For a period of time after hospitalization, he was sent for several weeks for physical rehabilitation.

Although we were not accustomed to displays of affection, I made it a point to give David a kiss good-bye when leaving from a visit. I am so grateful to have given these good-bye kisses to a man I had considered a son.

Shortly after his return from rehab, David passed from this earth in exactly the way he had wanted to – at home and peacefully. The details are not really necessary except to say that he told me just a few days earlier that he had wished to die at home and in his own bed. When he did not show up for breakfast, Tommy cautioned Koz to check on David and so Koz did so. David was found lying peacefully in his own bed on March 11, 2013.

His wake and funeral were as he had wanted – filled with friends and family, his beloved son and the love of his life and her husband. David approved of this marriage, saying that he was happy Linda would have someone to care for her. He had always been generous in his love.

The funeral Mass was said by Msgr. Frank with whom David played baseball when Msgr. Frank was a young curate and David was a boy. I was privileged to give the eulogy, not difficult because David was a good, kind and holy man. Ironically, the funeral luncheon was given at the Mustard Seed kitchen – at least for me, a sense of reconciliation was in the air.

David was buried not with his father as he had wished, but close to his father and with his grandmother. He belonged to someone. He belonged to all of us. Go in peace, dear David. We love you.

DAVID

O, strong one
Fearing nothing,
Fearing no one

My right hand
And my left

You loved Daniel
Above all
And Linda, too.

You suffered much
At the hands of many.

Beyond all, you were
A survivor.

Godspeed from the
Mother of the house.

MADELINE

There are only two incidents at the Mustard Seed that remain in my mind about Madeline. She was a dear, rather attractive woman of about sixty-seven years. I do not know if Madeline had children of her own, but for a time she was a mother at the Mustard Seed.

There was a child, a very young child, perhaps a toddler. His own mother had left him temporarily at the Mustard Seed to pursue whatever. Madeline took it upon herself to care for the child, and so she did, doing a good job of it. We were grateful to have her care until, finally, a more permanent residence could be found for the youngster.

The second incident involving Madeline was, in a sense, more personal to me. It involved, of all things, my own toothbrush. I happened to be in the bathroom one day and, looking up, I saw my toothbrush hanging above the sink as it had always been, yet dripping with water. I thought for a moment, and then….Madeline…… Coming out to the kitchen, I asked her, "Madeline, did you use my toothbrush?" Oh, I hated to hear that answer. "Ah, yes," she answered softly. "But I only used it for a little while."

At this point, I decided to assess my options: I did not speak any particular words of dismay or disgust. I could throw away the toothbrush and start over with a new toothbrush hidden from view…not an option. I had my reasons. No, I opted to rinse the toothbrush carefully and go on using it. This was my choice.

Although this was a rather comical event, it turned out to be a life-changing one to me. It was through this comic interaction that I gave my assent to the life at the Mustard Seed, accepting the Seed as it was, not changing it, not turning it in for a new one, but making do as it was.

The Mustard Seed was the toothbrush. My life there was to be accepted just as it was. And Madeline, dear Madeline, was the catalyst to help me see how I might live there in peace.

Mother (Madeline)

For a brief moment
You were a mother.

You nurtured.
You cared.
You protected, kept
The child
From harm.

You may have been
A mother before
Him.

We will never
Know – where were
Your children?

Were there?

We knew only one
We thank you for him
To us, he was your only child.

We wondered if
He savored the memory.

Lucky and Santa

THE LADY

The Mustard Seed hadn't yet opened as a house of hospitality when Lucky arrived on the scene. She was looking for George, a former priest staying with us while awaiting dispensation from his vows in order that he might marry. George worked for Catholic Charities at a shelter for men. (This shelter soon closed). Lucky, whose look can be described as exceptionally masculine, tried frequently to pass as a man in order to find a place to sleep, and George had joyfully announced to Lucky that indeed there was a place opening up where she would be able to stay.

And so, Lucky came and stayed. Thus began her long history as a member of the Mustard Seed community.

Lucky came and went from the Mustard Seed, sometimes staying at the House of Ammon. With her were some of her "Buddies", and among them, Bubba who often referred to Lucky as "The Lady" or "Lady Luck."

In the meantime, I, feeling quite battle-worn, left the Seed temporarily to join some Grail women in San Jose, California. I did not see Lucky again for more than nine months.

After this time I returned from California, coming back to the Mustard Seed and resuming my routine. On a certain day, I was walking through the dining room greeting the guests as usual. I came upon Lucky, said hello, and moved along. She followed me. "Wait, I have something to tell you," she said. We walked to Mrs. Fish's room where we could talk privately. Seems that Lucky had been away, too, to a half-way house in Rhode Island. There she experienced a conversion, had been talking to a priest friend and had stopped drinking. She had begun to drink when she was thirteen years old. Now she has stopped. She wanted to become a Catholic.

Later on, she was conditionally baptized – a Catholic. Michael and I were to be her godparents. For years afterward, we celebrated February 2 as Lucky's Baptism day. We became, in Michael's words, "the God family."

Things changed after that. Lucky and I moved to a room on Wellington Street, paid for with a small check that Lucky received from the government. I, myself, was totally without funds. Once again, I was cared for by the poor. We ate mostly spaghetti-o's from the food bank. And I learned a little more how it is that the poor can live.

My recollection of Lucky and my life with her over the next two years remains a little jumbled, but I write as I may remember it. There are some remembrances of our life on Wellington Street, but I will not tell them here, for this is Lucky's story, really. We later moved back to the Seed and more and more, I turned over my responsibilities to Lucky.

It has been said that a person's emotions stop growing at the age that they begin their addiction. Lucky began drinking at age 13 and in many ways, she was 13 years old when I met her.

I believe it was around this time that I had a major dispute with Michael and his companion. They were not at fault - no, it was due to Lucky's and my emotional immaturity. Sadly, there was little communication happening.

The sequence and incidents at this time remain in a jumble. At some point, Lucky and I moved to a small apartment on Russell Street. At this point, Lucky began to sink into a deep depression. If help was available, neither of us thought to seek it.

I recall two major events happening there: my friend, Pat, and I rather foolishly decided to attend a talk by a local warlock and then came back to the apartment. I began to feel the presence of someone else other than me, Pat, and Lucky (who was naturally hiding away in her bedroom). As I looked behind me out the second floor window, I saw the head of a woman with blonde hair and very red lipstick. Immediately shaken, I had an awareness of a woman who had been a friend of Lucky. The woman had died by suicide. Lucky had told me about her death, but had never described her. I gave Lucky a description of the woman I saw out the window. She agreed that it was that of the dead woman. I do not know if this could be true. Lucky was not in the best shape to discern. Given my own future mental health history, I could have been hallucinating, but something strange happened that night.

The next event was devastation. Lucky was suffering deep depression, and I had begun a friendship with a woman volunteer at the Mustard Seed. Although this friendship was short-lived, it tolled the death knell between Lucky and me. Her solution: back to the drink.

It was embarrassing to have to give up the apartment but it had to be done. Lucky had gone to the weeds, most likely, with her old street buddies. And I brought myself back to the Seed.

Time passed before Lucky and I could be friends again, but it did happen. Ultimately, I regained my position with her as both friend and godmother.

There were many incidents behind the scenes at the Mustard Seed. I had the infamous alienation from Michael which ultimately led to my psychotic episode. Lucky tried to care for me. I was away from the Seed for a while and then back. This finally led to my leaving the Mustard Seed completely.

Lucky maintained partial, but not complete sobriety. Also, there were difficult times on the personal level among some of us (me, Carol, Lucky). I was partly estranged from the Seed for some years and times were getting tough. Five years after my departure, Michael, too, took his leave from the Mustard Seed and headed for Sheep Ranch, California.

The reign of Lillian Clarke at the Seed, "the Lady", "Lady Luck" had begun. If nothing else can be said of Lucky, it was this: while she was "in charge", the poor were fed and cared for. To this day, some of the old-timers still speak of her goodness.

But there were other issues:

There was bullying, there was drinking, there were drugs. People took sides – for Lucky, against Lucky. Some went to the newspapers. It seemed that chaos reigned supreme.

In my mind, this was the darkest moment in the Mustard Seed history. In the meantime, Donna arrived on the scene. She felt called to work with the poor, and called to work at the Mustard Seed. I suggested she work around Lucky.

But wait, I have left out a very important piece – THE FIRE. During the time of Lucky's reign over the Mustard Seed, there was a huge fire, origin unknown, and the Mustard Seed House of Hospitality burned down. Fortunately, there were no deaths. Joe D. was seriously hurt but did recover.

The meal was served that very night in the back yard of the 9 Merrick Street property. A Mass was said after the meal and then appeared a huge double rainbow above both properties.

Days later, the St. Paul's Cathedral parish hall was offered for cooking and meal serving for the Mustard Seed. Donations for the Mustard Seed were received from throughout the diocese, churches, temples and others from Worcester County and beyond. The House of Hospitality was gone, but 93 Piedmont became a beautiful, state-of-the-art soup kitchen. Lucky was the over-seer for quite some time, but there were more difficulties ahead.

I had long since left the active ministry at the Mustard Seed. I believe it was the late 80's and I was working with developmentally disabled adults. There was a phone call. Lucky. She was ill. She had contracted the dreaded disease of AIDS. In those days, there was not much hope for survival from the disease, and Lucky was no exception. She stayed on living at the Mustard Seed property at 9 Merrick Street. David was her primary caretaker. Most were afraid.

In the meantime, I was asked to come to live with Koz and David upstairs and I, in my own little apartment downstairs at 29 Merrick Street - and I agreed. Oh, I had visions of Lucky coming to visit from down the street and my serving her tea on the back porch and taking care of her in this, her last illness. It was not to be.

On the very day that I moved in to #29, Lucky moved from the Mustard Seed House #9 to Mission Hill Hospice in Jamaica Plain. Donna had taken charge of the Mustard Seed soup kitchen. Lucky was dying. For nearly a year, she spent the week at the Mission Hill Hospice, and weekends with Koz, David, and me. As the time grew closer, and she was eventually unable to make the trip to Worcester, we made the trek on Sunday afternoons to spend the time with Lucky.

Late at night on October 24, David and I spent what was to be our very last visit with Lucky, who was by then unconscious. I did not stay to witness her last breath, telling myself that her caretaker was better equipped to handle such things. Truth is, I think I could not bear to experience the dying.

At 4:00A.M. on the morning of October 25, 1991 we got the phone call. Lucky was dead. The end of an era.

A funeral service was held at night on Lucky's behalf. Her two brothers, among others, were in attendance. Later in the month, we held a Mass for her at the Mustard Seed. Many were present.

Lucky was an enigma. Fr. Bernie often referred to her with the children's ditty: "When she was good, she was very, very good. When she was bad, she was horrid." Truth be known, this was rather an apt description of Lucky. Some loved her, some feared her, many were wary of her.

None could forget her.

Lil'

Lucky, dearest one
You were the girl
With the curl.

You were good.
You were bad.
But never indifferent.

Some of us
Loved you and
Were shocked to see
Your cruelty.

Some who feared you
Were shocked to see
Your goodness.

Many thanked you
For remembering your own
Abject poverty.

The weeds were
Home to you.

I have kept
Your mother's prayer plant.

Barbara

Barbara G. was a lady – a lady ravaged by alcohol, but nonetheless, a lady. She had class - and she was not about to let you forget it. I do not recall when it was that Barbara first arrived at the Mustard Seed. She did not arrive at the very beginning. If one were to look closely, you could still see that she once had been a real beauty, a "knock-out" you could say, with her long brunette hair (now graying) and her petite frame – drop-dead gorgeous!

I recall that Barbara came to live at the Mustard Seed sometime after Mama Bea established her reign over the third floor. Bea and Barbara became friends, chatting like school girls and drinking tea together in the afternoons. It is a wonder to me that the Mustard Seed measured up to her standard of living. Not every place did.

There is a story about how particular Barbara could be about where she might stay. It seems that she had been sleeping in the hallway of St. Peter's Church. The priest there, taking pity on her, allowed that he would rent a room where she might sleep comfortably. And so he did and so she did sleep comfortably – for a short while. Again, the priest observed Barbara sleeping in the church hallway. "Barbara," he asked quizzically, "what happened to the room that I rented for you?" "It had no curtains," she answered sharply. Subject dismissed. Apparently, the room was not up to her standards.

And so, we consider ourselves fortunate to have had her for as long as we did as our guest. I had difficulty with Barbara only once that I recall. I entered the Mustard Seed house to see Barbara seated on the front hall stairway. She shouted out an unkind word (about my size, I believe). I, displaying no goodness of my own, answered her back unkindly. I always regretted that exchange, but I feel that I got the chance to make amends soon after her death.

Barbara left the Mustard Seed of her own volition. I do not recall how I learned of her death – murdered, bludgeoned to death. I was asked to be one among several women pall-bearers for her. I was honored to be chosen as her pall-bearer, and I hope that it made up to Barbara for my short-tempered remark that I helped to carry her to her last resting place.

May you rest in peace, Barbara. May you be more beautiful than you ever were. Thank you for gracing our lives.

The Queen of Main South

Lovely lady
You were not
Dressed in blue.

All who knew you
Marveled at your
Lost beauty.

All who knew you
Wished for you
Only the best.

You suffered the
Worst for the
Death of you.

You were killed
In your kingdom.

You live now,
Forever,
The queen.

"Pray, Hope, and Don't Worry"

Gerard
(Photograph by Paul Gingras)

Gerard was not one of the live-in guests of the Mustard Seed...no, he came in another era. I first met Gerard while attending Mass at the Mustard Seed soup kitchen. He was a saintly man who, in those days, was in his seventies. I most recently learned something of his background: he was born the fifth of seven children and the eldest boy. I do not know if his childhood was uneventful but there was talk that his mother was "unable to care for him" and at some point in his life he was cared for by his sister, Marie Ange.

Gerard must have been a very intelligent boy. He won a scholarship to Assumption Prep School from whence he graduated with honors. He was a boarder there, coming home on weekends. There, also, he learned to speak French fluently. He is proud to say that he spoke French as if from Paris.

After graduating from Assumption Prep School, things seemed to go downhill for Gerard. He was ten years in a nursing home. This seems to be where the "mother couldn't take care of me," came in. Little else is known about that stay.

Next, Gerard spent ten more years in Worcester State Hospital. There are tales to tell from this stay. There were both a lobotomy and shock treatments. According to Gerard, neither approach was successful. What was successful, was a combination of certain medications.

All was not well for Gerard while at the hospital. He spoke little to none for his ten year stay. Apparently, he was hit or beaten daily by a fellow patient. Gerard said nothing. He told me that he just chose not to speak, but others have heard that he chose to imitate Christ by not retaliating against his detractors. Thus, Gerard was finally released from the State Hospital. He lives now in his own apartment, with limited supervision.

One last note about his family. Gerard is quick to say that he is like his father in that he loves books and, like his father, he is not handy.

Gerard is a humble man. He speaks mostly of God, the Church, and the saints. His favorite saint? Probably Padre Pio and, to quote Padre Pio, Gerard has so often given us the admonition, "Pray. Hope. And Don't Worry." Gerard has often told us that he was blessed with a good memory. I believe that he knows more about God, the Church, and the saints than most of us.

His humility radiates. "God's in charge. I wasn't meant to be in charge." "I have a special vocation", he says, but does not elaborate.

After years at the Mustard Seed Masses, Gerard was asked to be the altar server and he does his job well. Gerard is 85 years of age now. There are a few issues. Woe be to the one that even intimates disagreement with the Church. Gerard will then talk often and at great length, silenced only by the other turning directly away from him. Beyond these peccadillos, Gerard is thought by some, myself among them, to be a saint.

He walks weekly to the Mustard Seed, serves the Mass, when there is a Mass, and enjoys the company of friends. We are grateful for his service, his company and his friendship.

We thank God for his fine example.

Gerard

humble man
not meant to be
in charge.

above all
thinking of
God, the Church, the saints.

loving books,
blessed with a
good memory

suffering much
only in silence.

an inspiration
against our haughtiness.

some would call
you a saint

carry on, Gerard
Pray. Hope, and
Don't Worry.

The Professor

Bill was sometimes called The Professor. Whether he actually taught graduate or even undergraduate classes remains a mystery. He was very intelligent. If one dared not to recognize such a fact, Bill would see to it that you learned – soon.

He was a large man with a darkish, well-trimmed beard. Bill reigned over the second floor. People were invited to stay or to leave according to his whim. This prompted a wry comment from a short-term community member: "Oh, yes, there's the third floor, Bill's floor, and the dirt floor." The implication was no one was caring for the guests (the dirt floor), and everyone had staked out their own territory. I must say, I disagreed with this analysis. That being said, Bill certainly was territorial watching over his "apartment" like a mother hen.

There was tea for his special guests and gourmet dinners insomuch as he was able to scrape up the ingredients for them.

Despite his great intelligence, Bill was thought to be a drinker. I, myself, never saw this in him. And it was likely because of the drink that he landed at the Mustard Seed in the first place.

Also, he was a pianist, quite a good one we understand, though none of us ever heard him play for lack of a piano. So, there was tea, good food, beautiful music (records or tapes). The second floor was rather other-worldly.

Despite his commandeering of the second floor, Bill was a good soul in many ways. I owe him more than one debt of gratitude. He tried, oh how he tried, to teach me to sing and read notes. To, no avail. I had somehow missed out on the ability to learn. When it came to music, I thought Bill might be the ticket. He was patient and kind, but I could not learn. This was my last attempt at formal singing and music. I do not fault Bill for my failure to accomplish it.

As has been said in other narratives, there was a time of mental illness for me. It was Bill who arranged for me to see a therapist. I am grateful for this kindness.

Finally, the Christmas present. Bill printed out in calligraphy a beautiful oak tag piece – in Latin:

> *"Pauper sum ego*
> *Nihil habeo*
> *Cor meum dabo."*

> *"I am poor. I have nothing.*
> *I give my heart."*

How these words resounded in me at the time, living at the Mustard Seed. I was poor, had nothing, and hope that, at the least, I gave my heart. I kept this piece for many, many years until finally giving it over to a dear and trusted friend. I think this memento is one of the nicest Christmas gifts that I have ever received. I owe much to Bill, the Professor.

I understand that Bill was finally asked to leave. Drinking. But this story has a somewhat happy ending. Bill again found his way to a twelve step program and it succeeded. The sad part: some of us have run in to Bill on the street or in stores. Nothing. Bill seemed to want nothing to do with us.

We have not seen him in recent years. So thank you, Bill, and good luck to you wherever you are.

Bill

You were the professor.
The restauranteur.
Host for a day
Or an evening
One might say.

You could be brash
And sometimes
Were.

For others, only kindness.

All-in-all,
A good soul.

Some called you
Big Bill

We were made wiser
For having known you.

Lucky was escorted by the bullies

The Bullies

The Mustard Seed had not officially opened and yet there was a loud rap on the door. When I opened the door, there was a sight to see – a line of four men and one rather manly-looking woman. First was Lucky, about 5'9", in front of Bubba – taller, then Nutman - still taller, then Montana, the tallest, followed by Walter. Some might call Walter short and scrawny. I never really got to know little Walter because he drowned in Coes Pond shortly after this. These other men were the bullies.

Lucky, in particular, came looking for a place to stay since there were no quarters at that time for women in the city. She and the others frequently stayed in "the weeds" – an area near the Blackstone River where the homeless, often alcoholic, would bed down for the night. But the weather was becoming colder.

Bubba, Nutman, and Montana were Lucky's friends, drinking buddies, companions and protectors. The men owned two huge black Newfoundland dogs. I do remember one was called Moën. I always felt sorry for the dogs since they seemed to spend much of their time tied to the fence by the front yard.

The bullies spoke and those guests who were around, they listened….carefully.

There was one who was not afraid. That was David. Bubba was the most fearsome. The day came when Bubba, drunk, of course, gave David a push. David did not budge. In fact, he gathered his strength and pushed Bubba back. Bubba fell on the floor and later told David that this was the only time that Bubba had ever been knocked off his feet. There was respect for David after that.

As for the others, there was fear. Bubba was a bully even to those he liked. He liked me, for instance….called me Jeremiah; always spoke to me as "Jeremiah was a bullfrog." Bubba's greeting to me, however, was always accompanied by a loud and stinging crack on the back.

Although all three were her friends, I suppose of the three, Bubba, Nutman, and Montana, Bubba was Lucky's enforcer. The four often stayed at the Mustard Seed. They were difficult.

Undoubtedly, the most difficult bullying incident came when others of the community were out of the country on pilgrimage. Something happened to one of the young women guests. She appeared unconscious. I did not know, at the time, that she had been drugged and over-dosed. I took her to what was then City Hospital.

In the meantime someone whom I do not remember, came to find me at the hospital, telling me that there was a gun at the Mustard Seed House. I went there. This is the story that I later learned about the event. The man who gave the drug to the young woman was attacked by Bubba, who took out a gun and played the game of Russian Roulette, actually pulling the trigger with the gun against the head of the perpetrator. The man survived. No bullets. By God's grace, Nutman had emptied the gun of bullets (unbeknownst to Bubba), thus very likely saving a life.

The young woman, "Sunshine", was spared any injury from the drug overdose and she recovered. Apparently, the police had come. Bubba and friends were gone.

As frequently happens, the oldest and the weakest ones were left; the youngest and strongest escaped the police and any recriminations. It was, of course, not our policy to call the police, but we were extremely grateful that everyone escaped alive.

Bubba lived many years after this incident, but I do not remember his living with us at the Mustard Seed again. I am not aware of whatever happened to Montana. I understand that Nutman became sober and is now himself a drug counselor.

Lucky rose eventually to the "heights" of "director" of the Mustard Seed and eventually passed from this earth in 1991. You should know that the Mustard Seed was closed down for a brief time until the entire community returned. Some of the oldest and weakest stayed on with us as a family and the Mustard Seed began to rebuild.

Yes, there were bullies. I hope they find peace. They are all God's children.

Bubba

You were rough
Tough
Mostly evoking fear.

You nearly killed
A man
But for the
Wisdom
Of a friend.

You did love
However.

You loved
Lucky.

Proudly you
Proclaimed

"I never touched her."

Peter

Peter

When I think of Peter, I am reminded of the cartoon character Pig Pen. Peter was not unclean; nor was he surrounded by dirt. No, Peter was surrounded by, well, "things": especially he was surrounded by books, papers, and sometimes clothing.

To enter Peter's room was to enter into the realm of "things", sometimes waist-high things. Peter was what some might call a hoarder - a hoarder of what he certainly felt were the very important things.

I do not remember how it is that Peter arrived at the Mustard Seed. It must have been some time near its beginning. I do remember that he remained at the Mustard Seed long after I had left.

For some reason, perhaps because of his affinity for "things", he was asked to take charge of the clothing room. He was very good at this, and I am told that he would often be "finding" just the right piece of clothing for each member of the community.

As I think of it, Peter was somewhat of a gossip and enjoyed carrying tidbits of information from one to another.

And then there was Michael, who seemed able to do no right in Peter's eyes. I liken it to a jealousy between brothers. Michael accepted these criticisms with grace and Peter could be relentless.

I never heard these criticisms as lack of love for Michael, but rather as a jealousy on Peter's part.

I did not know Peter to drink while I was at the Mustard Seed. I could be naïve. I heard stories of his drinking in later years. I do not know, but I have doubt that Peter was a true alcoholic; I do not know, perhaps his drinking could be called opportunistic. I have heard that during one of these drinking bouts, that Peter was hit by one of the bullies.

I would like to take this place to physically describe him: a short, slight man with a mustache, possibly to cover what appeared to be a cleft palate. He also seemed to limp and have a somewhat crippled demeanor ---- ?? cerebral palsy perhaps.

Peter seemed quite intelligent, and who wouldn't be, so surrounded by all those books and papers. For all of these issues, Peter was a very good soul.

I owe him a huge debt of gratitude: as has been said, I suffered a mental illness while at the Mustard Seed. It was Peter, among others, who sat with me daily so that I might not wander away, or otherwise cause myself harm.

Peter has survived many years now, and, but for a little more gray, looks very much the same as always. He lives in the neighborhood of Michael whom I believe he still loves as a brother.

So, we thank you Peter, for all the good that you have done, for all the good that you still are.

Ad multos annos, Peter. May you live for many years.

Pig Pen

You are given this name
in jest, Peter
For you, like Martha, were
Busy about many things.
Like Martha, there was a
Kindness about you.
And a willingness
To do good.
You had issues with some
But you did not lack love
We miss you now that
You are away.
And we love you still
Like a brother.

Cathy

Cathy is an angel. She claims to have been around the Seed for nearly forty years. Some of this time was undoubtedly on weekends or furloughs while she was in residence at the Worcester State Hospital. For all of these forty years I remember meeting Cathy only a few years ago while the Mustard Seed Masses were being held at the 29 Merrick Street house.

Now, a little background on Cathy, told to me mostly by Cathy, herself. She never knew her parents, and lived most of her young life in Brooklyn, NY. She grew up in foster homes and graduated high school in New York.

At age 13 she took piano lessons and became what may have been an accomplished player though she plays no more.

She made her connection with the city of Worcester when working here in the summers. There are a few suppositions about Cathy. It has been said that she wrote the words and music to what has become a very famous musical. She said it was stolen from her. Could be. And if you prompt her, she may admit to having been at the famous Woodstock event. Wild.

Cathy says her mental illness was brought on by the awareness of the Vietnam War. She was admitted to Worcester State Hospital in 1969 or 1970 and remained a patient there until 10 or 15 years ago. She resides now in a program in an apartment with two other women.

Cathy gave birth during some of these years to two children. She has no contact with her children or her foster family. Except for her Worcester friends, Cathy is alone.

As has been said earlier, Cathy is an angel in our eyes. She gives so much more that she gets. And Cathy does get. She frequently begs for change after prayer service or Mass. Yet, she generously offers pastry goods to all, and she is free with her money to those who have less.

I have never met anyone more grateful than Cathy. She is probably among the most faithful in attending Mustard Seed events: Masses, prayer services, anniversaries, funerals. Cathy is present.

We love her as a sister and we thank you Cathy for being you.

Thank You

You bring coffee
On a Friday
Thank you

Pastry for all
Thank you

Cigarettes and
Dollars to those
In need.

Thank you for
All you do, Cathy

Thank you for
Walking the
Mustard Seed
Path
Together with us.

You are an
Angel.

Arthur

Arthur never lived at the Mustard Seed, but he frequently appeared at dinner when he was not a patient at the Worcester State Hospital. Arthur was mentally ill and fancied himself a doctor. He was often regaled in a white lab coat and carrying a doctor's medical bag.

Lucky and I had moved to a room at the Wellington Street Rooming House. Down the hall from us lived Arthur. On a particular evening we began to hear a terrible uproar! Crash! Bang! Crash! Lucky had street smarts and cautioned me to stay in our room. (No one was dying, after all.)

In the morning we heard Al, the kindly rooming house manager. Though, generally kindly, Al was very angry on this particular morning. The anger was directed at Arthur. "You broke down my door, Arthur." "But, I lost my key, couldn't get in." Words were exchanged. Explanations were attempted. But, in fact there were no clear explanations.

As has been said, Al was a kindly man. First came the threat: "That is it. You can't live here anymore." Silence. Then the truth. "I can't leave. No one else will take me." More silence. This was it, after all no one else would take him and Al deigned to keep him. And, to my knowledge, Arthur did stay on Wellington Street at least until his next bout at Worcester State Hospital.

Thank you, Arthur, for adding some color to our lives and thank you, Al, for showing what true kindness can look like.

The Doctor

You fancied
Yourself a doctor.

But the doctors doctored you.

May you live in peace
Now, Arthur.

In all you say and do.

Tommy W.

Tommy W.

Tommy came to us in the very early days of the Mustard Seed. He was "found" sleeping in Crystal Park by a service aide. He had walked or run away from his foster home, a farm. But first, about the service aide. These were somewhat of a cross between a lay person and a policeman. They carried no weapons. As far as I know, they did only good. The city of Worcester no longer employs service aides. A real loss because they were very helpful to the people.

To continue my story: one evening, there was a knock on the Mustard Seed door – a woman service aide, and with her, Tommy. Did we have a space to take this fellow in, she asked. We did.

Thus began a forty-year relationship with Tommy and the Mustard Seed. He was seventeen years old. Tommy has a remarkable story. My earliest recollection of Tommy's story began when he was only five years old. This was the beginning of his devastation. At this time, he was living with his natural parents.

It was near Christmas. Tommy was present when their father asked Tom's brother if he might give up his firetruck to Tommy for Christmas. Tommy noted the wrapped present, and wanting to know for sure if it was the beloved fire truck, he set out to "steam open" the present over the fire. He had recently seen his mother steam open a letter addressed to his father, and so, the stage was set. The present caught fire. Tommy, in his pajamas, also caught fire. His father, an alcoholic could not wake up. It was the downstairs neighbors who, hearing Tommy's screams, rushed in to save him. He was devastatingly burned throughout his body from neck to feet. It has been said that Tommy actually died and was resuscitated more than once.

After this, he survived a lifetime of surgeries and hospitalizations. As if this were not bad enough, Tommy's natural parents gave him up to foster care. As I understand it, he saw his mother briefly one more time. She hurried the visit so that the abusive father might not see him. As I understand it, since then, he never saw them again and has no idea whether they be living or dead.

There is a story, however, of a visit from the brother in their teenage years, of the brother urging Tommy to put on a sweater so as to cover up the embarrassing scars. After his first hospitalizations, Tommy remained in the custody of the State until his arrival at the Mustard Seed. Foster care was as usual, I suppose. Some placements good, some bad. Some, I understand, did not spare the rod. Tommy's schooling suffered. He learned some farming and animal husbandry, before finally leaving it all behind to come to the Big City – Worcester.

Life at the Mustard Seed was rather uneventful for Tommy as I recall, except that he was asked to leave four times by me. Each time, he returned. It was not that he did anything wrong at all, just that I thought he could make it on his own. I was wrong. Yes, he could make it on his own, but not happily.

I learned a great lesson from these comings and goings of Tommy. The lesson is this: if God wishes you to be at the Mustard Seed, you will be there – no matter who, no matter what.

As time passed, things got better. He was given cars as he needed them, and moved across the way to #9 Merrick Street House. He asked Koz if he would be able to stay at Koz's #29 house for three weeks. Of course, Koz was agreeable.

Three weeks has lapsed into many years. Tommy is content. He is a great asset to Koz's house. He lives now peaceably with John and Koz upstairs (with the cat) and me downstairs. Until recently, Tommy had become the cook – and a wonderful cook he was for all of us in the house – and sometimes to others as well.

Tommy was also my driver, since I am no longer able to drive. He extended himself, never refusing me or others this service in this, his latest car, given to him by Father Bernie.

Tommy is kind, if sometimes gruff. We appreciate his goodness.

He is our brother.

Tommy is ravaged by illness at this time. He rarely cooks and no longer drives. We miss these small kindnesses he so generously offers.

Addendum: Tommy passed to his eternal reward on March 10, 2016

Tommy

Scarred on the outside
Inside,
Purity.

You have learned
The art of
Silence.

You are generous
With your time
And your possessions.

The other day.
You brought me
Flowers.

Thank you,
Brother.

Herbie

I did not know Herbie. What is known of him was told to me by Margie, and, to a lesser extent, Michael. Herbie arrived at the Mustard Seed, brought by his wife who could no longer care for him. Yes, Herbie was dying. Margie and Michael agreed to take him in.

Except for his great, protruding middle, he appeared only as skin stretched over a skeleton. Still, Herbie was gentle and kind enough, and became fast friends with Margie.

"I'll take care of ya, Baby," he was wont to say. One wonders if he did. One wonders, "how could he," frail as he was. And one wonders if he takes care of her now, looking down on her from his place in heaven and we can hope only that he watches over us, her friends, from on high.

But, I digress. There is a bit more to Herbie's story than this. There was the trip to City Hospital. He was in great pain. Margie, who did not drive, walked with Herbie to the hospital to be treated. Upon arrival, Herbie was quickly put in a wheelchair. There was some, but not much, treatment.

Following is a little comic relief. It was at this or another hospital stay that Herbie, lying in the bed, visitors weeping spoke these words: "I'm dying, I'm dying... It won't be long now. I'm dying for a cigarette." Whether he ever got that cigarette is unclear.

Herbie wanted to be home in the 9 Merrick Street Mustard Seed house and so he returned, took to the bed. Marie and Joe, friends of ours and Catholic Pentecostals, came to pray over him. Then the death watch. Now, Herbie really was dying. Margie was present. Herbie breathed his last.

Immediately preceding this last breath, something amazing happened. Flying in the room was a beautiful butterfly. It floated around and landed directly on Herbie's chest. It remained there lying on Herbie for the entire time until the paramedics arrived for Herbie's body. After this, a few flutters, then out the window. We take this as a symbol of Herbie's resurrection and we hope that he continues to take care of Margie.

For all who knew you, we rejoice in your coming to the Mustard Seed, dear Herbie.

Herbie

I'll take care of ya, Baby

And may God take care of

You,

dear Herbie. Sick as you were,

You found the

Strength

To care for

One of us. And, how she

Cared for you,

Herbie May you now

Rest

Among the blessed.

Freddie and Debbie

It is unclear how Freddie arrived on the Mustard Seed scene. Debbie, a good friend of Tommy W., had been around the neighborhood for some time. She and Freddie were a couple and both moved into the Mustard Seed.

Debbie was a nice enough girl, rather quiet. It was suspected that Freddie used Debbie to work for him on the streets. It was a tough life. Freddie, a Vietnam vet, suffered from the ravages of war. He spared no one. The presumption, in addition to the ravages of war, was that he was drug-addicted.

They find themselves on these pages because there was a time when they ruled the Mustard Seed. Yes, they had taken over and violence prevailed. There was even a time when, in an unprovoked fashion, Freddie beat upon dear, sweet Michael who, in his typical non-violent fashion, refused to fight back. (Frankly, Michael was no match physically, for Freddie, anyway).

I knew neither Debbie nor Freddie very well and I believe they really took reign shortly before I left the Mustard Seed. But there are two stories that I remember well:

Debbie and Freddie implored me to take them to Hartford, Connecticut one fine afternoon. I did take them, but reluctantly, dropped them off and returned home. I returned to find that they had already made their way back to Worcester – ahead of me! I do not know, nor did I ask how or why they made the trip home with such alacrity. Thus was our life at the Mustard Seed.

The second recollection was regarding Freddie alone – an overdose. Freddie refused the hospital. I remember reminding him that he had the right to refuse but that as soon as he passed out, the ambulance would be called. Eventually, he was convinced to take the ride to the hospital. Richard and Michael went with him. Freddie survived. He continued his reign of terror.

Eventually, Debbie left. It is thought that she had a child and lives in a neighboring town. I do not know. Nor, to my knowledge, has she been seen in Worcester again.

As for Freddie, he, too, left the Mustard Seed, and none too soon. We last saw Freddie in the newspaper (not living in Worcester.) It seems he was fighting deportation – on the grounds that he had served this country well in Vietnam. He was pictured with a wife (not Debbie) and a child.

Freddie was a native of Scotland. We never learned what resulted from this endeavor to stay in the United States.

Good-bye, Freddie

Good-bye, Debbie

We hope that you have finally found a life of peace.

Freddie and Debbie

A cute pair, you made.

Pleasing to the eye.

But, a danger to

The heart.

You hurt us

Mightily.

A reflection of the hurt

That you must

Have felt.

You disappeared,

As you came....

Quietly.

We wish you only

Peace.

The Gun

Two men arrived on the sidewalk at the Mustard Seed door – one, a giver, one, a taker. I suppose it could be said. The "giver" represented an agency, a Christian shelter. Would we be able to provide a place to stay for the "taker?" (I do not remember the "taker's" name, let's call him Chris.)

We answered that, yes, of course we could house Chris. That was the end of it – and the beginning. The "giver" left, leaving Chris with us. It was all downhill from there. The day remained uneventful, but, oh, the evening.

I only remember walking up the stairs to the third floor kitchen. There, I found several people and dear Michael with a gun to his head – Chris. From that moment, everyone who rose to the third floor kitchen was held captive by Chris and the gun to Michael's head. Ultimately, there were eleven of us.

After quite some time, Chris decided to take Michael to the second floor. There were others there. We upstairs were nearly frozen with fear. Surely, we must have prayed but I do not have the recollection. I remember only that many had ideas to propose to me: trip him, hit him, etc. I refused these suggestions, not giving a reason. The reason was, however, that should these ideas result in failure, Michael could die.

Living on the second floor, thankfully, was an ex-Marine. When Chris arrived on the second floor with Michael, he was greeted by the ex-Marine. Wham! He knocked the gun out of Chris' hand. To the amazement of all of us, the gun was a fake.

Believe it or not, life returned to a fairly normal pace after that. I drove Debbie home, dearest Debbie, who weekly produced a hearty dinner – something out of nothing for the Mustard Seed, really. When I returned from bringing Debbie home – a surprise: Chris was sleeping in my bed! Where I did sleep that night I do not recall and surely, not in my own bed.

Chris stayed on for three days after the "hostage event." This, I presume, was the result of our compassion, our fear, or perhaps both. I believe he left the Seed of his own free will. There may have been some encouragement on our part.

Of all the difficult guests in the early days of the Mustard Seed, I may have borne the most resentment toward Chris. I think this appearance to threaten Michael's life may be the cause. I hope to be free of this resentment after all these years. The reality: we all survived to live happily. Hope you have done the same, Chris.

If there was blame to be had, we would want to blame the "giver" for the truth about Chris that he knew but did not share.

All is forgiven. We never saw Chris again.

"The Gun"

You threatened our lives.
A virtual threat, really.

We took you for
The real threat
That you appeared.

Your action allowed
Us to see
Michael's great strength
Of character.

You, Chris, you must
Yourself have been
In great pain to
Do such a thing.

We forgive you.
Forgive us our resentments.

Families

Volunteers

And

Catholic Workers

Aggie – Saving the Mustard Seed

Aggie was not a guest of the Mustard Seed House. No, she was a neighbor – a wonderful, irreplaceable neighbor.

A little history: Aggie, her husband, and daughter, Mary, bought their house on Piedmont Street in the mid 1940's. Aggie and her husband were in the restaurant business. Also, Aggie did housekeeping, worked in a laundry, and shoe factory. Aggie was a worker. When we met her, she was 59 years old.

To my knowledge, she never referred to herself as Aggie, but always Agnes. "And so, Agnes, I said….etc."

Her husband died in 1972. Aggie was a widow of two years when first we met her. She was generous and kind to us, her most unusual Mustard Seed neighbors. Frank recalls that every Friday, she sent over a large salad to be served at the dinner meal.

I remember that when Aggie had a particularly interesting story to tell, she would always do so in a quiet, rather whispery voice.

Ours was a reciprocal arrangement. Aggie was the best neighbor (just how great will be told shortly.)

John from the Mustard Seed helped Aggie with the yard and her dog – the men's work, so to speak. Mary, her daughter, had long since married. The story of Aggie and the Mustard Seed is one of how the middle-aged widow single-handedly saved us.

Here is the story which I did not learn until years after it took place: It seems that in the early days of our existence, there was a petition circulated among the neighbors. The petition demanded that our "operation" be closed down – a nuisance, I suppose. Finally the petition reached Aggie. "No, I won't sign," she allowed. "they don't bother me."

Now, Aggie was an abutter. Without the signature of the abutter, the petition could not go forward. And so, it did not.

Thus, the Mustard Seed went on for nearly forty years. Aggie, dearest Agnes, remains our hero for saving us.

Time passed. Aggie moved on in 1982, and we lost track of her – until recently when I encountered her daughter, Mary, in the neighborhood. Aggie lives!! She has reached the ripe old age of 98 years. We have visited with her a number of times now.

Yes, in some ways we must admit that she is ravaged by age, but she maintains that splendid personality, and we have come to love her as our own.

We do not forget her, and the great part she played in saving the Mustard Seed House.

Addendum:
Aggie passed from this earth on February 3, 2016 at the ripe old age of 101!

Saving the Mustard Seed

You were a stranger,
But only for a
Brief moment.

We became friends
For life

For the life of
The Mustard Seed

You welcomed us
You saved the day

You were strong
You stood up

It was you
Who welcomed us
The strangers

We thank you
Always.

Three Families

There were three families particularly dear to us in the early days of the Mustard Seed. Dutch and Helen were solid, middle-class folk. He, a banker and she, a church organist, they were salt of the earth types, living in a modest home on the east side of town. They raised three children. The eldest was Joanne, a nurse who had given up a formal nursing career to live and work with us at the Mustard Seed.

Joanne was sweet and lovely – most memorable about her: the day she single-handedly removed the maggots from an ulcerated wound of one of the guests. She was a gem and everyone loved her. She was the only person at the Mustard Seed or otherwise to ever call me Gerald.

Dear Joanne left the Mustard Seed, bore a son and I'm sure she continued to do good wherever life took her. Joanne passed from this earth at a very young age, cause of death a rare physical condition. We sorely missed her.

But this is not the end of the Dutch and Helen story. Yes, Dutch and Helen were most generous in supporting the work of their daughter and in supporting the work of all of us at the Mustard Seed. They were supportive of us in the humblest of ways. It was Helen, the banker's wife, who arrived weekly, mop and pail in hand, to clean the first, second, and third floor bathrooms. It was Dutch who arrived regularly with a huge box of toilet paper for the bathrooms.

Ah, Dutch and Helen were generous beyond measure. Mostly, they gave of themselves. We buried Dutch some time ago. Helen still lives.

We are grateful to both of them for their strong support for a few rag-tag youngsters who sought to do God's will.

Terry and Bernie were Mike's parents. They loved and admired him. They loved him so much that Terry was heard to say, "I really don't know how he was raised, I think he raised himself."

What I remember fondly about Terry and Bernie is that they worked part-time for a catering service. Weekly, they would bring food left over from their catering jobs to the Mustard Seed to feed the hungry.

They appreciated our work and were proud of their son who, at nineteen years of age, was a founder of the Mustard Seed House of Hospitality. Terry still lives. Bernie has passed to his eternal reward. We are grateful for all that they have given us.

Joe and Marie were beloved by all of us. For a long time, I had envied the great show of love and support showered on Michael by his parents. My own parents either ignored my work or were outright unhappy with it. I can almost understand why. I had left a successful teaching career to live and work, without pay, with the inner city poor. My parents had worked hard to send me to private girls' college and I suppose it appeared that I had ungratefully tossed it all away to pursue a dream. So, I felt the sting of non-support.

I have realized recently that when it came to the Mustard Seed, Marie and Joe were my surrogate parents. It was from them that we garnered much of our will to go on.

Marie and Joe were my friends from my early days of working with Catholic Charities. I lived with them three times in my adult life. They became immediately interested in our work at the Mustard Seed. Marie, who was less interested in the hands-on work, regularly donated food from their surplus to feed the hungry. Joe was literally, we felt, a godsend. If not for him, the dining room might have fallen through to the cellar – his bright thought to put lolly columns in the cellar to the dining room saved us.

Joe became the handyman and he was never so handy as when replacing windows broken out by young, angry, perhaps drunk or high, guests.

It would be more than one could bear to detail the patience, kindness and service of this extraordinary couple. We buried Marie to the strains of the beautiful hymn, "Gentle Woman."

Michael and I visited Joe in the nursing home only days before he passed to his eternal reward. We loved and admired them both.

And so, to you, Dutch and Helen, Terry and Bernie, and Marie and Joe, we send our gratitude. We do not forget you.

The Three Families

There were those who did not
Live with us.

They were essential
To the work.

Terry and Bernie and Marie
They offered things:
Surplus food
From the kitchen,
From the caterer.

Helen, you toiled and
Dutch brought the essential ingredients.

Joe, you gave the columns,
The windows, the skills.

All gave something
Above all you gave yourselves.

You gave to us who had so little,
Needed much
You were God's hands.
Thank you.

Joyce

Thunder Thighs

Joyce was a rather unusual girl. I call her "girl" because she was only fifteen years old when she first arrived at the Mustard Seed. (This was soon after we opened the house.) Joyce and her family lived on Austin Street, around the corner from the Mustard Seed. I do not know what caused her to investigate this Catholic Worker house, but she came and she stayed, often sleeping on the extra bed in my room more often than not.

When I speak of unusual, Joyce was tall, probably six feet one, and she had the maturity of one twice her age. Joyce did a share of the work and took on a job specific to her. In those days, Mass was said every Tuesday night, and this was thanks to Joyce who carved out the job for herself of scheduling each priest to say Mass. Soon, she and we began to know nearly every priest in the diocese.

Joyce loved also The House of Ammon, the Hubbardston Catholic Worker House, and particularly she loved the mother of the house, Jeannette. They were bosom buddies, you might say.

As time passed and Joyce graduated high school, she took a job working at the PIP homeless shelter. It was here, as far as I know, that Joyce first acquired the nickname, "Thunder Thighs" - not particularly flattering, but still rather cute. Seldom was she called by this name directly. No, it was a name that we all knew, but rarely used.

More time passed. Joyce moved into her very own apartment. She became a nanny to a doctor's children and a good and attentive nanny she was. She was rather industrious in picking up small jobs: babysitting, housesitting, etc. Although the future appeared to loom bright before her, this was not to be.

She came to visit me. (I, too, now had my own little apartment.) Joyce was housesitting at the time and she had many a tale of woe about the neighbors. I believed these tales at first, but as time wore on, the tales became more and more bizarre and finally, at the end of the day, it came to me: Joyce was suffering mental illness. The rest of this story is not so pretty.

Early the next morning, I called Joyce's brother. Ultimately she was admitted to Worcester State Hospital where she remained a patient for many years. (There may have been some back-and-forth, some in-and-out of hospitals, but ultimately it was WSH where we visited her occasionally.)

Part of her travels included a stay with Mike and his family. We were grateful for their having taken her in. Joyce suffered from arthritis and by this time, walking became quite difficult. Ultimately, no walking. Ultimately, a nursing home.

We visited Joyce often in the nursing home. I arranged for a variety of her friends to take us to visit her. Though there were some ramblings about the actor, Kevin Costner, for the most part conversation with Joyce was sane and sensible. Good conversation, good friends…life was good…for a while.

Beth, Joyce's sister-in-law, had warned me that Joyce did not have long to live. I did not believe. Until I got the call. Joyce had passed from this earth at a very young age.

There was a memorial service. Fr. Bernie was there. Her friends spoke well of her. My favorite part of the service was to hear young Greg, (Mike and Diane's son) play a special song of remembrance of Joyce.

Joyce was a special person. She grasped the life of the Catholic Worker in her youth. I don't think she ever let go. We give thanks for her service and her friendship.

Joyce

You were so young
Yet you were so mature
Perhaps you needed to be.

Your life so short-lived
You were old beyond your years.
Perhaps you needed to be.

Yet were you
Too young to say good-bye

You were friend to Mike and
Jeannette above all.
Perhaps you needed to be.

You left us too early.

Thanks for the memories.

Neil

Neil

Neil was the troubadour. He sang his heart out. He played his heart out. Everyone loved him. He was a free spirit. As far as I remember, Neil came to the Mustard Seed as a Catholic Worker from the House of Ammon in Hubbardston. Most particularly, he added light and love to the Mustard Seed House.

My favorite recollection of Neil was of him playing guitar and singing in the old Mustard Seed kitchen. Tom N. was dancing to the music in his wheelchair. Yes, Neil made even the crippled to dance. It was beautiful.

Neil had children. He was married to Mary, who bore him two daughters, Andrea and Catherine. Sometime before this marriage, Neil fathered a son, Jesse. Neil loved each of his children.

Alas, this minstrel, this love of our lives, our dearest Neil, was not to remain long with us on this earth. The last time I saw Neil, he came to my house, helping me to fix a car. He left at 4:00pm. By 9:00pm, Neil was dead – apparently leaving my house to go to the hospital. I did note that he had a pallor about him, white, very, very white – otherwise, he maintained the same good nature as was his custom. He died, we were told, of a cancer, or something resembling it. We do not believe that he knew himself to be so deathly ill.

Neil was Mike's best friend. On the day following Neil's death, I learned a rather ugly truth about the poor.

Neil and Mike had traveled across the country together and were very fast friends. Now, Neil was dead, Michael in mourning.

All of a sudden, footsteps...one of the beloved poor, looking for Michael and finding him, uttered the famous words: "Can I talk to you a minute?" Michael graciously put aside his mourning for the time and tended to the man's needs. And I learned a difficult lesson. Ah, yes, the poor can be relentless in their want or need.

Now, for quite some time before his death, Neil had been looking for work. Finally, he approached Carol, the manager of a gas station. Success, a job!

As a symbol and a message to Neil beyond the grave, Carol slipped the set of keys to the station into his casket. Nevermore would he be without a job.

Goodbye, our beloved troubadour.

Neil

You were our
Troubadour
Loved by all.
You helped even
The crippled
To dance.
You left too soon.
Thank you for
Adding
Light
To our
Lives, Neil.
Thank you for
Being most
Uniquely
You.
We will always
Remember you.

Sherman and Pat – the Wedding

Sherman and Pat

Sherman and Pat were, and still are, our great friends – that is, they were great friends to me and to Michael, separately and together.

First, let me speak of Sherman, whose given name is Richard, the name he now likes to be called. But in those days, it was Sherman. As far as I know, he first acquired the name when he and Mike were in seminary with the La Salette Fathers.

"Sherman" was a cartoon character, somewhat stocky with glasses – his mode of transport was called "the Wayback Machine". Richard earned the name Sherman for his similarity in looks to the character, and once he arrived at the Mustard Seed, his bright yellow car was naturally called "The Wayback Machine."

Sherman, being out of work for a time, made the decision to come to Worcester to help his friend, Michael, at the Mustard Seed – and a great help he was. Sherman became the Sancho Panza to Michael's Don Quixote, full of love and support if becoming a bit critical now and then. Sherman sometimes referred to Michael as "Woodsy," as in, "You pulled another stunt on me, Woodsy."

Richard (Sherman) was solicitous not only of Michael, but of me as well. He and I traveled very briefly to Maryhouse, the Catholic Worker in New York City. Richard could not have been more fun to be around. It so happened that we arrived on a sweltering hot day. We walked around looking for bookstores with a bag of ice which we held on our heads. He was good and kind and lots of fun.

Eventually, he met Pat at the Mustard Seed. Pat was my friend from North High. Both of us taught there until she left to pursue a Ph.D. at Cornell, and I eventually left to pursue a different kind of learning at the Mustard Seed. It was Pat whom I visited weekly, mourning and weeping about the troubles at the Mustard Seed.

Pat was the type of friend whom one would hope for – a listener, not a director. Pat gave me cars. Oh, did she give me cars – every time she bought a new car (which was often enough) she bequeathed me her old one. For this, I will be forever grateful.

For their friendship, we will be yet more grateful.

Pat and Sherman remained friends for seventeen years! They waited, and they waited, and they waited. Then, finally, a marriage – to each other. They have been married for many years now. They are, individually and together, a rare find, a lasting love.

Pat and Sherman

You two were an unlikely
Match
At first glance.

Sherman, or is it
Richard?

You were a loyal
Friend to Michael.

Pat, you were a loyal
Friend to me.

All-in-all
We became
Friends to
Each other.

We thank you for
The friendship –
For being you at
A time when we
Needed you.

Koz

"Mad John" Ingraham, Michael and Koz

Jeanette often spoke of Koz as Saint Joseph. His quiet demeanor, his strong work ethic – The Good Provider - for all these, he earned the name.

As far as I know, Koz was introduced to the Catholic Worker through Father Bernie, who was at the time a curate at one of the parishes in Koz's hometown. Koz grew, entered the Navy, left the Navy, attended the University of Mass and left the University of Mass.

After what may have been one or another false starts, Koz, Fr. Bernie, Jeanette and others founded the Catholic Worker farm, the House of Ammon. Here the Saint Joseph analogy really came into play. Koz was a worker. Everyone knows that if there is one thing that every Catholic Worker house really needs, it is a good worker. Not only was Koz a good worker, he was a good worker who did not talk about his working.

Father Bernie and Jeanette loved Koz and continued to love him through the end of their days. Koz, for his part, remained associated with the House of Ammon for the seven years of its existence.

He remains always the worker offering his services to many. He is especially generous to the Catholic Workers here in Worcester, but I judge him generous to all.

As for his quiet demeanor, he is known for it. One last thing to be said about it – perhaps Father Bernie said it best, "He (Koz) would not tell you if your shirt was on fire." He was the silent type.

I know Koz to have a strong prayer life, but he would not like to have it spoken of here.

Many years ago, (over 30), Koz bought a 3-story house just around the corner from the Mustard Seed. Many of us have called this lovely place home, some for shorter periods than others. I, myself, have lived in Koz's house for these past 26 years.

Koz has been associated with the Mustard Seed now for many years. He was a plumber (now retired, so to speak), and has done much for many. It is with gratitude that I write these few words of this generous soul, our Brother.

Koz

To Jeanette, you were
St. Joseph

Generous and
Prayerful

Silent and
Kind.

From all who have
Benefitted
From your
Kindness

Let this be our
Thank you
To you,
The silent one.

Margie

Margie

Margie was a gem. I really mean a gem. She shines with the light and is priceless.

She arrived at the Mustard Seed in the early to mid-seventies, on the way to Madonna House where she hoped to become sober. She stayed. Yes, Margie is an alcoholic. Drinking or sober, she was beautiful, sober now for nearly thirty-four years! Margie was what was called a Catholic Worker kid. Both her parents, Mary and Arthur, were CWs of the first generation, contemporaries and friends, among others, of Dorothy Day and also Catherine Doherty, founder of Madonna House Apostolate in Combermere, Ontario.

Margie knew the Catholic Worker and "fit in" well to the Mustard Seed. Eventually, she and Michael became a couple, but this companionship was short-lived, though the friendship has lasted many years.

Margie was kind and loving to all and I have never heard her utter an unkind word. She seemed to practice St. Therese's mandate and the principles of Madonna House, that is, to do little things well for Christ.

Probably, she was the closest Mustard Seed friend to Herbie, walking him to death's door with him promising, "I'll take care of ya, kid." And we hope that he will take care of her from heaven.

Aside from her loving care of the poor, there were the wildflowers, bunches of lovely wildflowers brought back to the Mustard Seed after her frequent jaunts to downtown Worcester. There were difficulties also, but not of Margie's fault. I was jealous of Margie and Michael's relationship. This, along with my deteriorating mental health, led to my leaving my residence of the Mustard Seed. Margie, too, eventually left the Mustard Seed. She lived a most interesting life.

At some time during her earlier Mustard Seed experience, Margie found a mentor and became an accomplished weaver for Holy Rood Guild at St. Joseph's Abbey, weaving for years until back problems prevented her from weaving further. Later, she worked with college students teaching horseback riding.

Among her most interesting accomplishments was Margie's life tending sheep as a hermit - a life of prayer and subsistence living which she lived for ten years in New Hampshire, an inspiration to all of us.

Margie did return to Worcester, now and then. It was on one of these visits, a celebration for Father Bernie, that she was nearly killed – a car accident after the celebration. She had headed to her brother's home near Boston. This accident caused immeasurable harm to Margie, not the least of which was the loss of her right eye. As far as I can determine, Margaret accepted these infirmities with grace and dignity.

Later, came further caregiving. Margaret cared for her infirmed mother for the next fourteen years until Mary's death just a few years ago. Finally, a return to the Worcester area. We are so happy to have her near us.

We know that God continues to have plans for Margie and we bow to His will for her, hoping only that she remain among our dearest friends.

Thank you, Margie, for your continued inspiration.

Margaret

You hold us all in prayer
You, a caregiver.

One may think you were
Born to care for us
The poor, the infirm,
The weary.
The beaten down by life.

Are we not poor?
Are we not infirm?
Are we not all weary, and
Beaten down by life?

You, too, have walked
This walk
But
You show as you are shown,
The way
Of the Master.

Michael

Michael Boover

Fr. Bernie regarded Michael as a saint. In my mind, if Fr. Bernie thought of Michael as a saint, he likely is one. For me, personally, I have pretty much regarded Michael as a moral (Catholic Worker) compass. This has been all the more the case since the death of Fr. Bernie. While others may not agree, for me it has always been Michael, despite that I am ten years his senior. I have always looked to Michael for leadership and, I think, he sometimes looked to me. Yes, we were a team in our beginnings.

I first met Michael when he was nineteen years old. He was still a student at Worcester State College. Even his own mother found him extraordinary.

At 19, Michael signed the ownership papers for the Mustard Seed House and I followed him. The first five years were hard. I left. The second five years, wherein Michael held on valiantly were impossible. During these, the early years, there were beatings, broken windows, takeovers by a young and sometimes hostile (drug and liquor induced) element. There were hospital visits, and much, much more. For several months Michael was jailed for a nuclear power plant protest. I was still at the Mustard Seed at this time. All the while, he held to his non-violent principles and held on by his fingernails to the Mustard Seed House.

After ten long years, Michael left the Mustard Seed. In a sense, as with my own departure, he left our beloved Catholic Worker house, feet first.

Yes, the first ten years were hard.

After the Mustard Seed, Michael traveled to Sheep Ranch, a Catholic Worker community in California. Eventually, he recovered, healed, and gained strength. He came back to the area, no longer to live at the Mustard Seed. Instead, he rented a tiny house set in the middle of a field – adorable, a house for a solitary life.

Somehow, he met Diane and after a courtship, took her for his wife. It appears to be a good match, still together after twenty-nine years. There are four beautiful children: a daughter and three sons, all adults now.

Michael earned his D.Min. and for a number of years taught at a small Catholic college in the area. Currently, he is a chaplain at the Worcester State Hospital. He keeps up the Catholic Worker tradition at their beautiful city farm with meditation groups in their "Hound of Heaven" chapel, monthly Dorothy Day reading groups, and other Catholic Worker oriented events.

He still seems to love and care for the Mustard Seed as though it were his own child. At times, it is still difficult. Michael occasionally speaks of himself in a somewhat self-deprecating manner. He is "a rascal, a marshmallow, a cosmic cupcake." To us he is a love, still a leader, still the moral compass, still the light on the path.

Thank you, dear Michael.

Michael

"Marshmallow
Rascal
Cosmic Cupcake"
These you call yourself
But I, I call you
Compassionate,
Courageous
A visionary of sorts.

Thank you for the
Many years of
Friendship
Overcoming obstacles,
Victorious friends

How sweet
To know you.

May there be
Many more years.

Frank

The White Knight

Frank was the White Knight. He earned this fine nomenclature, bestowed by me, for his willingness to be called on in any emergency. He was good and kind and appeared fearless in the face of danger or difficulty.

For most of the time of the life of the Mustard Seed, Frank lived with Brenda in a separate apartment in the area. There was a period when Frank and Brenda did live in the Mustard Seed, but it appears that time was short-lived – too much for Brenda, it seems – and who could blame her?

Frank was a founder of the Mustard Seed store front and (later) House of Hospitality. Though he did not live in the house for long, he supported us financially and otherwise. I can still see him on the front porch. I can still see him laying out one hundred dollars on my hand to help run the Mustard Seed. The fact that Frank did not live with us caused some consternation, and I'm afraid the difficulty was much of my own doing. I'm afraid I caused some pain to Frank by my refusal to consult him in the serious decision-making of the Seed, and by my inability to see what an integral part he still was in the life of the Mustard Seed. It has taken all these many years to finally begin to make amends for such a colossal oversight.

Aside from the White Knight moniker, I always thought of Frank as the Universal Lover. Frank loved nearly everyone and nearly everyone loved Frank. In fact, I do not think there was a woman, gay or straight, who met

Frank and did not fall in love with him. In fact, he was at least once heard to say, "All we really have to give is love."

He also spoke of loneliness and how he came to the Mustard Seed to ease his own loneliness. Frank was uniquely adapted to Mustard Seed living. Coming from a large family in Chicago, he would frequently leave his home to seek refuge and silence amidst the crowded silence in the streets. He knew how to find peace among the crowds.

Frank's family were descendants of the tiny country of Luxembourg and Frank, not Francis, was his given name. As you might imagine, he was handsome beyond measure – in the early days and now. His long blond hair flowed below the waist – and to this day, he wears a signature handkerchief in his back pocket.

Frank left college to pursue anti-war activities. He took a job working for the Worcester State Hospital and later, the railroad - all very hard work from which came the money to support the Mustard Seed. About this time came the founding of the Mustard Seed house and the moving, moving, moving. I sometimes think that Frank moved half the city of Worcester in those days.

When he was not working at Worcester State Hospital or on the railroad, it seemed he was moving households and on Friday nights, serving beans and hotdogs for the meal at the Seed.

So often people came looking for Frank at the Mustard Seed. He was not there. But he was very much responsible for its underpinnings. Ultimately, Frank had less connection with the Seed and married his beloved Brenda. It should be noted that it was Brenda who supported the Mustard Seed in her own quiet way, and it was she who ultimately financed much of the workings of the Seed.

Frank and Brenda became parents to two lovely daughters, Kendra and Alexandra, both adults now. Sadly, Brenda passed away several years ago leaving Frank, a widower.

Frank, like most of us, has slipped away from active ministry at the Mustard Seed only to return to spearhead plans for the future life of our beloved Mustard Seed. He has worked for many years as a Christian community organizer.

We have known him now for over 40 years. We love him.

The Universal Lover

You love many and
The many
Love you.

You, the Christian
The Buddhist.

You, the lovely one
The lonely one

You, the White Knight
Coming to save the day.

Thank you for
Being a part of
Our heart.

For saving the day
Your light
Dawns again.

You are
A Love.

Geri

MUSTARD SEED OPENING

Geri with then Fr. Frank Scollen and
Jeanette Noel

Opening night at the Mustard Seed –
March 25, 1974

The Abbess

I was the Abbess. This was the title Fr. Bernie bestowed on me. I did not like it. In my mind, an Abbess is one who sits on her dais and barks orders to her underlings. No, I never liked being called the Abbess. This mattered not a whit to Father Bernie. To him, I was still the Abbess.

I came to the Mustard Seed Catholic Worker by way of Madonna House, a lay Catholic community headquartered in Combermere, Ontario. I had been visiting the community for three weeks and had just decided that I might ask to stay on there for another year when I was abruptly asked to leave. I did never know, nor was I ever told, the reason for my being invited out of the community. I suspect it may have had to do with my lesbian leanings. To my knowledge, I did nothing to suggest that I might act on them, though.

But God sometimes writes straight with crooked lines. Catherine, the foundress, called me aside as I was leaving and gave me the rather dubious directive, "Go to Dorothy Day. She takes all kinds." And so I did call Dorothy when I returned to Worcester, and Dorothy instructed me: "Usually the young volunteers come to New York, get a job and an apartment then give service at the Catholic Worker."

I thanked her very much, hung up the phone and thought to myself, "Certainly not." I then got a job teaching in Worcester, letting go of my directive to go to the Catholic Worker. At the school where I was assigned to teach, I met my teaching assistant, Daria. I spoke often of community and my desire to found one. Daria knew just the men I should meet, and introduced me to Frank and Michael, Catholic Workers. The rest is history. Literally.

After the storefront, the Mustard Seed House opened on March 25, 1974. Michael and I moved in, previous to the Grand Opening. We took in many guests in the early days and some came to live permanently. Again, for me, the first five years were hard.

In November, I left the Mustard Seed for a 9-month respite, living with women from the Grail, an international Catholic women's organization. My closest Grail friend, Veronica, worked with Cesar Chavez and the United Farm Workers Union in California. I was privileged to participate in the UFW march to Modesto. I could have stayed in California. Veronica had asked me to be her assistant.

But I was missing "home" and returned to the Mustard Seed in the following September. Things happened. For me, the difficulty came not so much with the guests, though there were problems. No, the difficulty came with relating to the workers. Also, I think my prayer life was not as strong as it perhaps could have been.

My problems increased exponentially. I so much regret my treatment of the relationship of Michael and

Margie. I have forgiven myself my transgressions and thankfully, they have forgiven me.

Finally, a breakdown – my mental illness. Charlie, Mrs. Fish, and Peter took on the job of "watching" me for a month. After this, a recuperative stay with Marie and Joe, followed by a stay with my parents and then back to the Mustard Seed.

Finally, I left the Mustard Seed for good – no more to reside there, but interested, always interested. For the last twenty odd years, my Mustard Seed task: to thank the donors. I do so gratefully to be able to participate in some small way in the work. Upon leaving the Seed, I took some small jobs (at a pharmacy and at a hardware store).

For the following fifteen years I took a position as caregiver for developmentally disabled adults. Because of this work, I hope I have learned the lessons of helping to assist those I care for in living a life of peace and quality. After these years, I was encouraged to leave my work, disabled by mental health. I was down, but not out, so-to-speak. Again, God writes straight with crooked lines.

My widowed mother needed care. I was free now to care for her, and I did so (and she for me in a sense) for the seven years preceding her death. This was accomplished in my apartment. After this, there was exercise and the joining of a 12-Step program which likely changed my life. I still live at the house around the corner from the Mustard Seed, still send thanks to the donors to the Mustard Seed Catholic Worker, and am involved now with others in the CW community in addressing its future needs.

For me, the life of the Mustard Seed has been both very challenging and supremely joyful. My association has lasted now for these forty-plus years. I suppose I have found my community. Only God can truly discern. I thank God for the opportunity of living such a life.

Alleluia.

The Reluctant Abbess

I was the
Reluctant Abbess

I did not want
To be.

I could be
No other.

Did God
Call me?

Was Catherine right
All along?

Does the Catholic Worker
Take all kinds?

I hope so.

Alleluia

Father Bernie

Father Bernie – Mass at Saint Francis

and

Therese Catholic Worker House of

Hospitality

I did not like Fr. Bernie when first I met him. I thought he was most inhospitable. He did not introduce himself to me, nor did he ask my name or even offer me a chair. How rude.

But the Mass. Oh, that Mass!

We had left Worcester from the Mustard Seed storefront – the first beginnings of the Mustard Seed community. I had just met Michael and Frank, co-founders, and I, being interested in founding a community, was introduced to them.

It was customary for us Mustard Seed people to make the weekly trek on a Sunday to attend Fr. Bernie's Mass at the House of Ammon Catholic Worker community founded by him and others. Now I know that a Mass, is a Mass, is a Mass, but Mass at the House of Ammon was special. The music was beautiful, but the reverence of the priest was beyond inspirational. He became mentor to some in our journey as we left the storefront and purchased 93 Piedmont Street, the original Mustard Seed House.

Our pilgrimages to Sunday afternoon Mass continued until fire took the House of Ammon and its community seven years after its inception. From the Mustard Seed storefront later emerged the purchase of the house of hospitality, serving a live-in community and practicing the works of mercy.

Fr. Bernie became more and more our spiritual advisor and I, who had basically disliked the man, was happy to talk with him about what had become for me a crisis of conscience. A mutual friend brought us together. I soon began to love him, and thus emerged a twenty-one year history with him as my confessor. Also, he began to say Friday night Masses with the Mustard Seed community, and this relationship lasted until his death in 2011.

Yes, there was always the Mass, the beautiful Mass.

There were many things I found enviable about Fr. Bernie – a major one, his dealing with the poor – difficult for me to explain – a bit paradoxical. He somehow related as an equal without condescension, yet he spoke in all his dealings with the moral authority which we knew to be his. He was their friend, generous with his time, attention and money, as well as with all his possessions.

And, too, he lived with and surmounted both his demons and his challenges. I have had concerns that some would think him "hatched" a saint. But, no, he surmounted his demons and faced his challenges.

As many know, he was a celibate gay man. He speaks of this issue in the book written by his friend Rosalie Riegle Troester, Voices from the Catholic Worker. How difficult it must have been to be a gay man of his generation.

And, yes, he was a recovered alcoholic, sober for nearly 50 years, all the while helping those who still suffered. He also suffered bi-polar illness – yet, he carried on with great hope.

No, Bernie was not hatched a saint, but he loved God and trusted in God, and tried to take many of us along with him – the rich and the poor, the worthy and the unworthy.

The Mustard Seed goes on, yet we endure the great loss of him. It was not, however, a Mustard Seed person that characterized him best for me. No, it was an older parishioner of St. Anne's who said in speaking of him, "He was my best friend." And yes, I thought to myself, "Ah, yes, he was your best friend and a best friend to all."

He was a good and holy man. We pray for him and, we pray also to him.

The Priest

Love God.
Trust in God
You urged this
Always.

From Abbie
You learned
Love of people.

You walked the earth
With courage.

There were those
Who did not love you.

I did not know them.

We loved you beyond measure.

We are reminded of the
Loaves and fishes.

It was you, dear Bernie,
It was you who were the kid
Who gave all he had.

The Mustard Seed Tree by Rita Corbin

Epilogue

I hope that I have accurately depicted the people and places in this endeavor. Some have been inspiring and some have conspired to wreak havoc. All have their place in this little story of a moment in the long history of the Mustard Seed.

Donna has left the active ministry at the Mustard Seed, though she still serves the poor. Others have returned to carry on the work. We are happy to be doing so.

The Mustard Seed continues, now a soup kitchen served once again by some old timers and others, the Saints and the Rascals – bless us all.

     Geraldine DiNardo is a long time Catholic Worker and a foundress of the Mustard Seed House of Hospitality. She grew up on the shores of Lake Nipmuc in Mendon, Massachusetts and attended Saint Mary's High School in nearby Milford. Geri received a B.A. in Sociology from the College of Our Lady of the Elms in Chicopee, MA and a M.Ed. from Worcester State College. Geri travelled to Madonna House in Combermere, Ontario, to explore vocational tugs to faith, service and community. Returning to Worcester, she worked at Catholic Charities and later taught in the "Drop Out" program helping high-risk adolescents at Worcester's North High School. Geri then joined the Mustard Seed Catholic Worker Community as house co-founder and leader where she started her own home repair co-op in the early days and took up subsequent labors of love at the neighborhood drug and hardware stores where she could remain close to the neighbors she loved. She also worked for many years with developmentally disabled adults in the city. Geri has been long inspired the 19th century Utopian Christian visionary, Adin Ballou, who founded the village of Hopedale near her hometown. She remains admirably persistent in living out the Catholic Worker vision and is an esteemed member of the growing community of Mustard Seed elders who are still at work but who are also seeking to share the Catholic Worker torch with a hopeful younger generation.